Ghosts and Hauntings
of
Ventura County

"I don't believe in spooks, but I'm scared of 'em all
the same."

--Mark Twain

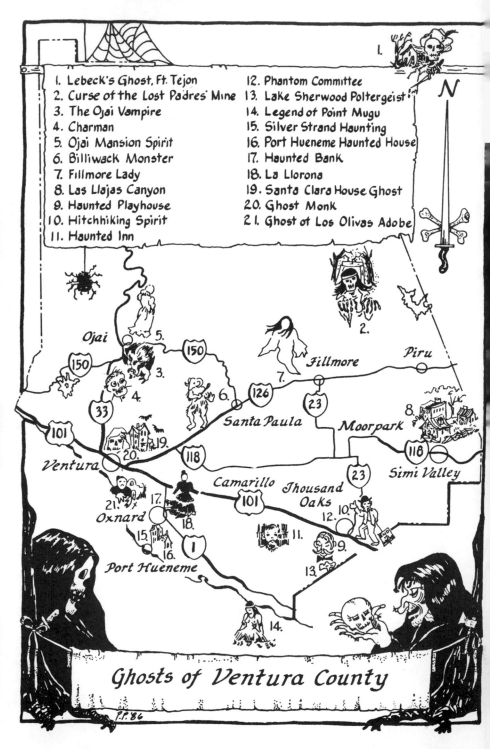

1. Lebeck's Ghost, Ft. Tejon
2. Curse of the Lost Padres' Mine
3. The Ojai Vampire
4. Charman
5. Ojai Mansion Spirit
6. Billiwack Monster
7. Fillmore Lady
8. Las Llajas Canyon
9. Haunted Playhouse
10. Hitchhiking Spirit
11. Haunted Inn
12. Phantom Committee
13. Lake Sherwood Poltergeist
14. Legend of Point Mugu
15. Silver Strand Haunting
16. Port Hueneme Haunted House
17. Haunted Bank
18. La Llorona
19. Santa Clara House Ghost
20. Ghost Monk
21. Ghost of Los Olivas Adobe

Ghosts of Ventura County

TABLE OF CONTENTS

Ghosts and Hauntings of Ventura County   1
    Ghost Map of Ventura County   2
    The Ghost Monk of Mission San Buenaventura   3
    Santa Clara House Ghost   7
    Dark Lady of the Olivas Adobe   9
    Charman   13
    Ojai Vampire Tale   16
    Haunting of an Ojai Mansion   19
    Spectral Sheepherder of Wheeler Canyon   21
    Billiwack Monster   21
    The Haunted Inn   25
    Georges   28
    Phantom Committee of the Conejo   31
    Poltergeist at Lake Sherwood   33
    Westlake's Disappearing Hitchhiker   33
    Haunted Ghost Town of Las Llajas Canyon   35
    Fillmore Lady   36
    Curse of the Lost Padres' Mine   38
    Ghosts of Fort Tejon   41
    Apparition of La Llurona - the Crier   45
    Something Is Watching Us   47
    Silver Strand Haunting   52
    Haunted House of Port Hueneme   54
    Legend of Hueneme (Lady of Mugu Rock)   55

Ghosts and Hauntings of Santa Barbara County   59
    Ghost Map of Santa Barbara County   60
    Hector, the Ghost of Summerland   61
    Three Nuns of Ortega Road   65
    Black Fisherman of Santa Barbara   67
    Hope Ranch Poltergeist   70
    Ghostly Children of Santa Barbara   73
    Ghost Lady of Santa Barbara College   76
    Crying Child of Mission Santa Barbara   78
    Ghosts of Las Cruces   79
    The Haunted Hacienda   81
    Ghosts of La Purisima   84
    Black Coach of Santa Ynez   90
    Haunted Tavern of Guadalupe   93

Ghosts and Hauntings of San Luis Obispo County   95
    Ghost Map of San Luis Obispo County   96
    Black Lake Lady   97
    Alice, the Ghost of the Rose Victorian Inn   100
    Captain Cass's House   103
    Ghosts of Mission San Miguel   105
    Ghostly Lady of Adelaida   108

Ghosts of the Channel Islands   111
    Ghost Map of Channel Islands   112
    Cabrillo's Ghost   113
    The Haunted Islands   115
    Chinese Ghost of Santa Cruz Island   116
    Footprints of Prisoner's Harbor   118
    Santa Rosa Island Ghost   120

Conclusion   121
Glossary   122

ACKNOWLEDGMENT

The author wishes to thank the following for their help in compiling the better known haunts of Ventura, Santa Barbara, and San Luis Obispo Counties: Jane Gilbert, Lee Harris, Dr. Cyril W. Anderson, Charlie Seamann, Ann Snider, John Chan, Sharon Detwiler, Rita Reimert, Dawna Burnigham, Pat Salazar, Tom Graham, Regina Graham, Gayle Emmons, and Nadean Peterson. Special thanks to my wife Debbie Christenson Senate.

Many thanks go to Eugene D. Wheeler for book layout and editing, Patricia Pedersen for her drawings and illustrations, Robert M. Howard for book cover graphics and typeography, Spectrum Office Services for typing, and Lou Hartney and Eugenie G. Wheeler for proof reading.

INTRODUCTION

In legend, literature, and film the long abandoned, decaying mansion on the hill has been the common image of the haunted house. The cobweb encrusted, dank and dark Victorian is firmly established as the typical haunted house, but this image, though having some basis in fact, is far from reality. Many haunted houses are newer buildings. Even brand new tract homes without previous owners have been found to have special "guests." Some haunted houses can be light and colorful, modern and tastefully furnished.

In general, haunted houses are normal everyday homes that for some reason have become disturbed by something paranormal. What triggers the disturbance may be someone in the house, a past event or some change in the site.

The most common experience reported in a haunted house is that of footsteps or muffled voices. The sounds can be loud and seem to come at set times. The footsteps may be heard on the same route, such as the clicking sounds of women's high-heeled shoes heard at one haunted house. The footsteps would walk up the cement walkway to the front door. Then a tapping would be heard. When the door was opened, no one was there. The second most common experience is that of apparitions--images of individuals seen moving through the house. These experiences are, for the most part, very quick glimpses of the paranormal. In one home a man was viewed in the bathroom. On investigation, no one was there. At other times the bathroom light would mysteriously turn on.

Certain features seem to repeat in many haunted houses. Staircases, bathrooms and bedrooms are common sites for ghosts to wander. Many of these sightings report the ghosts as being very much like living persons: not transparent, but seemingly solid. Their only consistancy is the odd habit of vanishing!

Lights going on and off, doors opening, pictures falling off walls; these are also events that are reported in haunted houses. These events can be terrifying. Objects move around, screams are heard, invisible hands touch people, icy blasts are felt, and fires burst out on their own. These and other horrifying events can cause a family to panic and abandon a house in terror.

In 1978 my search began for the ghosts and hauntings of the Gold Coast (Santa Barbara, San Luis Obispo and Ventura Counties). Since then I have collected a mass of information on the colorful and lively specters seen in many of the Gold Coast's aged buildings and on its deserted roads.

These stories are only a sampling of the many cases I have on file, but they reflect the more dramatic encounters with the unknown. Some of those interviewed are prominent men and women in responsible positions who want their names withheld. I have kept confidential the locations of many haunted buildings to preserve the privacy of their owners.

Ghosts have been with man since the dawn of history. All cultures in the past and present report seeing them. The evidence is too massive to ignore.

The Ghost Monk of Mission San Buenaventura

A sudden chill raced down my spine as I slowly approached the massive adobe and stone mission church. The Moorish tower loomed stark in the steel gray winter sky. I had selected the old Mission San Buenaventura as the starting point for my search for Ventura County's ghosts. A gray-robed specter of a monk has been reported seen at the mission for years. The streets were still damp from a sudden winter shower as I climbed the steps to the garden. I had an appointment with someone who had encountered the apparition of the monk.

The courtyard was empty, peaceful, relaxing. It is difficult to imagine what it must have been like in the days when Ventura was under the Spanish flag. The Mission had been established in March of 1782 by Padre Junipero Serra. It was the last mission the good Father established. He died in Carmel two years later. The present church was constructed by Indian laborers and completed in 1809. Damaged by the great earthquake of 1812, it was repaired in 1815 and since then has served as a house of God. Unlike many of the old missions of California, San Buenaventura is not a reconstruction. It is the original structure built by the Franciscan friars. A century ago the Mission was the center of two dozen adobes that formed the village of San Buenaventura. The phantom monk's appearance may indeed date back to that earlier time.

As I waited in the garden, I reflected on those timeworn walls. So many groups of people had walked where I now waited; padres, Indians, rancheros, Mexicans, and Americans. I could sense that each had left his psychic mark upon the location. It is no wonder that so many accounts of ghosts and phantoms are linked to this site.

I was soon joined in the garden by Mrs. S____, a longtime Ventura resident in her mid-fifties. She wore a long coat over her short figure, and her reddish-gray hair was tied under a scarf against the wind. I noticed at once the intensity in her eyes. She had been aware of her psychic ability since the age of six. It had been several years since she had witnessed the ghost monk at the Mission. We shook hands and she walked toward the ornate side door of the church. She stood about five feet from the door. "It was here," she said. "I was standing here, after leaving the church. I had just lit a candle and was about to leave when I stopped here."

3

She had been having troubles with her family and had gone to the church to pray for guidance. "I saw the figure come from around the back," she continued. "It appeared solid. It was as real as you are now. It was a man, perhaps in his fifties, I think, gray hair. He was dressed in a loose fitting robe. It was gray in color and tied at the middle." She believed he was a member of some monastic order visiting the historic mission.

I asked her if there was someone else in the garden at the time who might have seen the monk. She was certain that she was alone. She said that she felt a distinct chill as the figure slowly came towards her. "I did not think of him as a spirit. As he came closer, I could feel a sense of warmth and concern coming from him. He smiled at me and disappeared."

When I questioned her about the figure's position when it had dematerialized, she pointed to a spot about ten feet from the place where we were standing. I paced over to the place and stood for a moment on the spot. Perhaps it was the cloudy weather or my own imagination, but I felt a definite chill on the spot and an intense feeling that I was being watched by someone or something behind me. I glanced back. We were alone.

Mrs. S_____ and I retraced the route which the phantom gray-robed friar had taken back to the rear of the old mission. Today a small monument stands, dedicated to the three padres who are buried within the church. Mrs. S_____ firmly believes that the kindly apparition she encountered that afternoon years ago was the spirit of one of those padres. She took the phenomenon to be a positive sign that her problems would be solved and her prayers answered through the intercession of the pious monk. She informed me that within a month her problems were resolved. The woman never felt fear when she saw the phantom. She sensed that he wanted to help her. "I would not mind if I saw him again," she said.

Now, whenever I visit the mission, I feel there may be a presence around the aged walls.

There are other accounts of encounters with the ghost monk of Mission San Buenaventura. Interviewing a member of one of Ventura's oldest families, I was told that the ghost had been seen around downtown Ventura for generations. The figure, seen late at night, seemed to be keeping some kind of appointment. I asked if she knew why the phantom walked the earth. She seemed to know but, sensing that she may have said too much, refused to divulge more. My curiosity was piqued and I pressed her to tell me more. She seemed to blush and said only that "he did something monks are not supposed to do." Whatever his sin, the good monk has been trapped by it for decades.

Others tell of encountering the monk on Main Street and even by the banks of the nearby Ventura River. He was seen in peaceful contemplation. The Mexican and Spanish residents of old Ventura considered it highly unlucky to see the phantom monk.

An interesting footnote to the ghost monk is that in the stories he is reported to be wearing a gray robe. The Franciscans wear brown. They gave up the gray robes decades ago!

A monk arrayed
In cowl, and beads, and dusky garb appeared,
Now in the moonlight, and now lapsed in shade,
With steps that trod as heavy, yet unheard."

Lord Byron
Written upon seeing the
Goblin Friar ghost.

The Santa Clara House Ghost

I stood outside the Santa Clara House, now a restaurant on Santa Clara Street in Ventura. My attention was riveted upon the round window on the second floor, for it is believed that the ghost looks longingly out that window. I saw no figure looking out that night. I walked up the stairway to the main entrance. The old Victorian home had been made into a family style restaurant, but it retained the charm and elegance of the last century. A group of students from my class in Ghosts and Hauntings had reserved the upper room for an end-of-class banquet--a dinner with a ghost.

I had been to the Santa Clara House several times, but had never been to the upper chamber. The hostess, a pretty young woman, informed me that my party was already upstairs. I was escorted up the old staircase. I paused for a moment. These stairs were reported as the focal point of the haunting. I saw no apparition as I mounted the stairs, but I reflected upon reports of patrons at the restaurant who saw a lady in a long dress on the stairs. Also I recalled how one of my students' children had pointed at the staircase and asked who the beautiful lady was. There was no one visible on the stairs!

In the dining room the rest of my group waited, among them several who were psychic. We toured the upper floor and the excitement of the evening seemed to enhance our "ghost hunt." Several of the waiters and waitresses had encountered something on the upper floor. The management helped out by having one of those who had encountered the spirit, Rosa, come and tell of his experience.

The most dramatic encounter happened to a young waiter as he mounted the staircase. He looked into a mirror and saw not his own reflection but the face of a young woman with a strangely elongated neck. She was wearing a fancy dress of the last century. The waiter was frightened at this odd vision. An interesting element is that the waiter is of Italian extraction and legend claims that Rosa the phantom is also Italian.

In the latter decades of the Nineteenth Century many Italian families moved into Ventura County. Rosa was the daughter of one family. Forced by the pressures of that day into a loveless marriage, Rosa became unhappy. Her husband, a man much older than she, was frequently out of town for weeks. Her frustration ended when a young Italian man came to Ventura.

They had much in common and soon became lovers. She became pregnant--a condition that could only confirm her husband's suspicions of infidelity. Her lover was away in San Francisco and Rosa spent many days at her window awaiting his return. The young man never returned.

The story claims that in desperation Rosa tied a rope around a beam in her room and placed a noose around her neck. As she stepped from the stool, her family arrived. They heard the stool fall over. Rushing in, her father quickly cut her down, but they were too late. She had broken her neck and died on the floor. The legend states that this occurred in the Santa Clara House, but research indicates that a Rosa never lived in the house. Rosa could have died at a nearby house, but her ghost shifted later to the Santa Clara House.

Suicide is a prime cause of the wandering haunt. It is almost as if the act of self-destruction dooms a soul to wander the site of its last desperate act. Several in our group felt a sudden chill as we were told the story of Rosa.

We discovered that the women's bathroom on the second floor seemed charged with energy. The stairs were also singled out as charged with psychic energy. We learned that some of the waiters and waitresses do not like to go to the upper room alone and will work there only in pairs.

We also discovered that the restaurant management did not like to use that upper room, preferring to use it only for special banquets or when the rest of the establishment is full.

From several sources I learned that another room in the Santa Clara House seems to be haunted. The red room--just off the staircase--is said to be charged with a strange presence. One psychic lady reported seeing a sad image drifting through the room!

Some believe the legend of Rosa is just a tale but those who have felt her presence realize that the Santa Clara House is more than a restaurant. Because the bar of the house is a recent addition, it is clean of psychic disturbance. The only spirits found there are in bottles.

The Dark Lady of the Olivas Adobe

In Ventura the two-storied Olivas Adobe stood stark in the red sunset. Dark and foreboding, the windows seemed to stare at us as our group gathered to search for the ghostly lady of the Olivas Adobe. As our team of psychic researchers started to arrive, I pondered the long history of this historic building.

The adobe was built by Don Raimundo Olivas in the mid-Nineteenth Century and served as the main hacienda of a large Mexican rancho. Don Raimundo had grown wealthy during the gold rush of 1849. He drove his herds of cattle north up the San Joaquin Valley to the hungry miners of the Mother Lode country. Don Raimundo's profits were immense, and with his fortune he built the two-storied adobe house.

The hacienda is large; it had to be, for Don Raimundo and his wife, Teodora, had twenty-two children! Guests also stayed at the adobe for as long as they liked. Fiestas were held at the rancho that lasted for days on end with wine, food, music, and dancing.

I wandered from the parking lot into the grassy courtyard. The sun was vanishing over the horizon and the lofty trees cast dark shadows. The grounds of the old house are peaceful now, but they have known violence in the past. In 1855, the hacienda was robbed by a gang of bandits. Stories claim that the outlaws took seventy-five thousand dollars in gold from the Olivas family. The bandits struck Senora Teodora Olivas and ripped the gold earrings from her ears!

Legend holds that a posse was quickly formed, which gave chase, and some of the outlaw gang were caught and hanged--but the gold was never recovered. Some believe the bandits buried the loot somewhere between Ventura and Santa Barbara.

Another tale claims that Don Raimundo saw the gang approaching the house and gave his strongbox to a trusted Indian servant to bury. Don Raimundo stalled the bandits as they searched the adobe for gold. Finding none, they paused to tear the earrings from Dona Teodora's ears and then returned to their horses. As they were about to leave, they saw the Indian servant with a shovel.

Believing he was attempting to attack them with the tool, one of the bandits shot him dead. Only the servant knew where the strongbox was hidden and he took its location with him to the grave. Many treasure-hunters have searched the grounds around the adobe seeking the lost wealth, but to no avail.

Tales of treasure did not bring me to this site. It was stories of a ghostly woman that caused me to form a group to study the historic adobe. Several people reported seeing "a dark lady" standing near the kitchen. A gardener years ago saw a lady in a black dress inside the house while he was trimming shrubbery. Upon checking, he discovered no one was there! One of the tour guides at the hacienda told of hearing piano music coming from the living room. When she checked, there was no one there. Others have encountered odd smells and strange footfalls on the balcony that could not be explained.

I rejoined our group and began our ghost hunt. Two people felt a watching figure from the second story of the house. One man touring the courtyard felt that there was once a graveyard in the corner of the walled court. A quick check with the historical interpreter confirmed that a small graveyard had indeed been located on that site decades ago.

Many had distinct feelings but the major opinion was that there was no ghost at the house. Those who visit the historic home are not allowed into the rooms and can view them only from the doorways. This evening the historical interpreters gave us special permission to enter the rooms.

Mrs. P_____ was skeptical of the tales of ghosts at the house and felt little on the grounds of the hacienda. She was about to leave when I urged her to at least tour the inside rooms. As soon as she entered her eyes grew large. There was a sudden tenseness in the air. Another of our group felt a moving presence. Mrs. P_____ started walking from room to room. She seemed drawn to the sewing room. As she entered, she saw a woman in a black dress and black hair standing in the corner of the room. Mrs. P_____ felt anger coming from the figure. This dark form slowly vanished. Others also felt her presence.

Mrs. P_____ felt that the dark lady was in fact the ghost of Dona Teodora, the wife of the builder. She lived nearly 50 years at the adobe so it is only logical that she left a psychic trace in the old hacienda. We departed with new respect for the tales of ghosts and hauntings reported at the Olivas Adobe.

Tell me not in mournful numbers,
Life is but an empty dream!
For the soul is dead that slumbers,
And things are not what they seem.
--Henry W. Longfellow
A Psalm of Life

If I saw it, it might be a ghost and it would scare me
badly because I don't believe in ghosts.

--John Steinbeck
Cannery Row

Charman

At night Creek Road near Ojai can be a dark, foreboding thoroughfare with huge oak trees looming on either side in threatening stances in the moonlight. Few homes dot this lonely stretch of the winding road. I wondered why I was driving this depressing road in the middle of the night. But whenever possible I try to visit the sites of places reputed to be haunted. As local tradition contends that the ghost known as Charman is seen on this road late at night, I knew I must visit the place in the evening.

Charman, the ghost of the Ojai, is perhaps one of the best known spirits in Ventura County. People say that he walks at night, the ghost of a man horribly disfigured by flames. Many trace the origin of this legend to the great forest fire of 1948. It is believed that he was a fire fighter caught when the wind changed, sending a wall of fire over him. In flames he ran into the forest and his body was never found. Because he was never given a proper burial, he was doomed to wander certain roads in the Ojai at night. Research done by Charlie Seamann, former curator of the Ventura County Historical Museum, debunked the 1948 fire theory--for records show that no one died in that massive blaze. Another story of Charman was related to me by Miss K_____, a resident of Ojai. "He is the ghost of a man badly burned in an automobile accident. He was so badly burned, he ran into the woods and died. Many in the Ojai have seen him."

All of the stories of Charman agree on one detail. The apparition is hideously disfigured. His flesh peels from a burned skull. Charred rags are all that remains of his garments. Some have even reported a sickening smell accompanying the apparition. The specter is said to lunge out of the darkness and attack those unfortunate enough to be walking Creek Road at night.

As informants were mostly young people from the local high school, I classified Charman as a typical "Lover's Lane" ghost. It seems that those places designated as Lover's Lanes attract tales of bizarre ghosts. I suppose it is fun to get together late at night after a football game and drive the lonely road, searching for the ghost and telling horrible stories. Not bad entertainment; certainly better than watching T.V. or doing homework.

Originally Charman was believed to wander Shelf Road, but that was before it was developed. Once lights were put up, it lost its dark and mysterious atmosphere. It was at that time that the ghost moved to Creek Road.

Many years ago, in the 1950s, a few newspaper stories were published about an alleged attack on a young man by Charman. A jacket was torn from the teenager by a mysterious figure. The articles caused a traffic jam as young people from all over the county converged on Creek Road to see the ghost, to the consternation of the local police.

As Charman has been seen near the bridge by Camp Comfort, I drove past the darkened park and stopped near the bridge. The air was cool and my breath steamed from my lips. The quiet was broken only by the sound of the creek below. I got out of my car and walked to the bridge. I felt very alone out on the bridge late at night, armed only with a weak flashlight.

It was easy to imagine how people, after spending an evening telling ghost stories, could become convinced that every branch was a specter, every owl a spirit. Hallucination can be a powerful thing.

Does a horrible ghost wander Creek Road at night? Perhaps, but Charman did not make his presence known to me that cold night. I was relieved that he did not appear.

Creek Road is rumored to hold other phantoms besides the hideous Charman. People have encountered the spectre of a ghostly horsewoman riding at full gallop along the road in the moolite. She rides to a curve in the road where the horse was spooked by a snake and she was killed by the fall from the animal. She re-enacts the tragedy on the anniversary of her death.

Another apparition is a ghostly lady in a wedding dress who is believed to hitchhike along the road. She is said to be the phantom of a young woman murdered on her wedding day. Recently the ghost of a headless motorcyclist, riding an old **Indian** bike, was encountered, roaring along the highway. He is the most recent addition to the ghostly inhabitants of Ojai's Creek Road.

Ojai Vampire Tale

There is a legend in the Ojai that seems to belong in one of those horror films produced for afternoon matinees decades ago. It is a tale of a vampire who terrorized the valley around the turn of the century. It is believed by some that the stone casket of the vampire is still visible and that it holds the corpse of the creature. The vampire is rendered harmless by a stake driven into its heart. But, so goes the tale, do not remove the stake, for to do so will loose this awful horror on the countryside.

The vampire arrived in the late 1890s from Spain or Italy, so says one source. He bought a ranch, not a large one, just for a place to stay. Soon after his arrival a number of cattle were discovered slashed and drained of blood! There followed attacks on people by strange, wolf-like creatures. Once the ranchers of the valley realized what they were faced with, they knew what course of action to take.

They knew the creature did not travel by day, being forced to stay in his casket. Searching the lands of the newcomer, they discovered the ornate stone sarcophagus by a crossroad off Creek Road. But the vampire realized his helplessness in the daytime hours and had a huge black dog guard his casket. This ferocious devil dog would rival the celebrated "Hound of the Baskervilles." The creature kept the ranchers away from the grave until one of the intrepid vampire hunters realized that the huge black dog was a thing of evil and as such was repelled by the sign of the cross. Producing a large silver crucifix, they advanced toward the snarling, barking canine. The dog retreated before them. As they found the stone sarcophagus beneath a tree, almost concealed by tall weeds, the dog sensed danger to his master and charged the group. Several Winchesters fired with no effect. But, as the terrible creature drew near, a rancher sprinkled a vial of holy water taken from the old mission upon the beast and it retreated, whining in pain.

It took several moments to pry the lid from the casket, but more time to build up the courage to drive home the killing stake. They sprinkled the remaining holy water upon the vampire's body and placed a cross upon his chest. Fearing to do more, they replaced the lid and left as the sun was setting. The Ojai has not been plagued by the undead since.

The great and terrible dog has been seen several times on Creek Road, and some say that they have found the stone casket above the ground and hidden by weeds. They claim that the casket has a window in the lid so that, by clearing away the dirt and dust, one can peer into the sarcophagus and see the skull of the Ojai vampire.

The lurid tale may be more than simple folklore. There may well be a nugget of fact hidden within the fable. Some of the older families of the last century did bury their dead in family plots on their own lands. And, it is not unlikely that a wealthy rancher might be interred in an above-ground sarcophagus--an old European concept where frozen soil in winter or swamp conditions made burial in the earth difficult. The use of a window to look upon the dead would also not be too unusual in the last century.

So a casket in the weeds may exist. The existence of the grave does not prove the existence of the vampire. The story may have originated when kids out hiking stumbled upon the grave site and speculated about what it was. The tale of the guardian hound of the vampire has a history that might reach back to the time of the Chumash Indians. The Indians believed their Shaman, or witch doctors, could change themselves into fierce animals, usually black in color. These terrible apparitions would attack those of the tribe who had broken sacred tribal taboos. The Indians may have imparted these beliefs to the early Spanish settlers who translated them into the European concept of the vampire. The entire tale may be a corruption of far older native American religious beliefs.

Still, Creek Road can be a foreboding place at night and, if you should find an almost hidden casket in the weeds, do not investigate too closely. Whatever you do, don't take away the stake that keeps the vampire bound to his grave!

The Haunting of an Ojai Mansion

The wave of cold suddenly flooded into the large dining room of the old mansion in Ojai. It was the first indication that a ghost was present. I had been asked to lead an investigation of the large house by the present owners. They had experienced enough problems to know that a ghost hunter might be useful. I had gathered a large number of people to help in the investigation. The afternoon had gone by without serious psychic disturbance. Now, as the sun set, the mansion seemed to be coming alive. As the cold entered the room, I rose from my seat to determine from where this mysterious temperature was emanating. Everyone was feeling the presence of something out of the ordinary.

I was assisted in this investigation by a gifted psychic and psychic researcher. She could feel the presence of a woman. She sensed her leaving the dining room and going down a long, dark hall into the huge living room of the old building.

With hairs rising on the back of my neck, I followed the cold into the chamber, armed only with my ever-present flashlight. The temperature in the huge room seemed to drop ten degrees. The sensation of such cold on a warm summer night was unnerving. The room seemed empty. Moonlight shone into the chamber through large windows. I caught something out of the corner of my eye. I glanced down a long corridor and saw a dark shadow materialize. The psychic standing behind me saw the apparition also. Other brave members of the team filed into the room and watched as the figure of the woman moved away from us down the corridor.

The image was wearing a long dress of the last century. For two breathless minutes the apparition was visible. Slowly it faded away. As it vanished, the room started to return to normal. Six investigators had witnessed the materialization. Each of us confirmed what the others saw. All agreed as to the size, shape and type of dress.

We then examined the corridor to see if the apparition was caused by a reflection or shadow. No tree outside the window or mirror in the hallway was present to explain the dramatic event.

The ghostly lady may well have been the wife of the builder of this elaborate building. She was never happy there and perhaps her sadness has filled the atmosphere with her vibrations.

Whatever we saw, it was enough to convince both skeptic and believer that the house was indeed haunted.

The owners of the house have sold it. Perhaps these new owners can dispel the sadness of the ghostly lady.

Spectral Sheepherder of Wheeler Canyon

North of Ojai twists lonely Wheeler Canyon. For years legends of a spectral sheepherder were told around blazing campfires. It is believed that a poor basque sheepherder was murdered by ruthless cattlemen in the last century. Hatred between sheepmen and cattlemen was commom throughoutthe American west. The history of California is blotted with several bloody incidents between these warring groups.

I was first told of the phantom sheepherder by a group of boy scouts who had hiked into Wheeler Canyon and camped for the night. The scout leader told them the story of the murdered shepherd and how he was seen late at night on the hillside surrounded by spectral sheep--still haunting the site of his murder.

At first I believed it was a typical fireside ghost story told to frighten young campers. Then others began to relate the tale to me, older residents of the Ojai Valley as well as psychics. It appeared that the awful murder had left some sort of "psychic scar" on the land and that the crime is replayed over and over again.

> "And who are you?" cried one agape,
> Shuddering in the gleaming light.
> "I know not," said the second shape,
> "I only died last night."
>
> Thomas Bailey Aldrich

The Billiwack Monster

A blood-red August moon was low on the horizon as Miss J_____ and I drove the twisting, turning road up Aliso Canyon a few miles north of Santa Paula. The two lane road was dark, and I hoped my car was in good condition because a mechanical failure or blow-out would be most unwanted now. Miss J_____ knew well the story of the monster and had agreed over the phone to tell me about the mysterious creature. We had agreed to meet at a cafe in Santa Paula. I found Miss J_____ to be an attractive professional woman in her mid-20s, with long brown hair and a winning smile that was sure to put strangers at ease.

"You believe in ghosts?" she asked, as we sat down in the small cafe. "Yes," I answered. "I do not as yet know what they are, but something exists that people refer to as a 'ghost.' I know because I have seen several things which I could not explain." She seemed relieved. "I'm glad," she said, as I brought out my portable tape recorder. I try to use a recorder whenever possible to preserve exactly what is said in an interview.

"Many people think you're crazy if you start talking about spooks," she smiled at the word "spooks." "Not spooks," I corrected her. "Ghosts, haunts, specters, or phantoms, if you please, but not spooks. In fact we psychic researchers prefer to call them apparitions." "I don't know if this thing is a ghost," she said, after ordering some hot tea. "It might be something else."

My interest was high now. I had heard of the Billiwack monster for years, but I assumed it was only a tale told to frighten children. Now the expression on her face was that of deadly earnest. "Have you seen the thing?" I said, trying to use a normal tone of voice. She nodded, "I saw something."

Before she would continue the narrative, she asked if I would like to go "up there." I agreed at once. Finishing our tea, we took my small foreign car up Aliso Canyon to the site of the abandoned Billiwack dairy. As we drove, she gave me some background information on the old dairy. It had been built in 1925 by a man named August Rubel. He dreamed of a modern dairy designed to be a model of efficiency. The stock market crash of 1929 ended his dream. It was abandoned in 1943.

August Rubel was a mystery himself. He vanished on some type of secret mission for the army in North Africa in 1943. His disappearance was never explained. From that day on, the old silos and concrete buildings acquired legends of ghosts. It was not long after its abandonment that the first reports of the monster were recorded.

The monster is believed to live in the hills around the old dairy and wanders the ruins at night. It is described as huge with powerful muscles. Its body is covered with gray or off-white hair. Its fingers are tipped with long talons. The monster's face resembles a goat or ram with horns on its head. It has been described as a "great hairy man."

As many of the sightings have been made by young people, the local authorities have written off the monster as a prank or just over-imagination. "I was in high school, a junior, when it happened," stated Miss J_____. I tried to keep my eyes on the road, searching for some sign of a club-wielding monster. "It was sort of a game with us--searching for the ghost of Rubel at the dairy or talking about the monster. Nobody really believed in the monster story--it seemed so far-fetched." In the darkness and the rural stillness I was not so sure that the tale was all that far-fetched.

"We drove up here. There were five of us that night. We had some beer but we were not drunk. We had been up by the old dairy and were driving along this road. We are almost there now." I was near the end of the road, hopelessly unaware of where I was. "Here," she said. "Stop here." I pulled over to the dirt side of the road and turned off my engine. The quiet was overpowering; crickets chirping in rhythm was the only sound. "This is as close as we can get now to the old dairy. They have watchmen now with guard dogs. I can't take you there now, but you see over there." She pointed to a fence almost overgrown with weeds. "I saw the monster there. We were driving down this road. My headlights flashed onto it. It was horrible! It had eyes like a cat's--shining in the headlights. It just stood there--with a head like a sheep and a body like a man. Its hair was coarse and matted. It was there maybe twenty seconds and then it took off, running. I saw it. It ran away on two legs like a man! I was so scared I didn't know what to think. Some of the people in the car thought it may have been a stray ram or some kind of joke. But it seemed real!"

I got out of my car and, in the moonlight, walked with Miss J_____ to the fence where she had seen the man-beast. I asked her what color were the thing's eyes. "Greenish-yellow," she said. I must admit that I started to feel watched out on the road. She too seemed ill at ease and by mutual consent we quickly returned to the car.

As we reached the vehicle, I heard a rustling in the brush near the fence. I have never seen two people enter a car and push the car door locks faster than we did that night. Our intruder waddled out of the brush in a nonchalant manner, giving us only a glance. It was a large possum crossing the road. What a relief!

What is the monster? A relative of Bigfoot? A spirit of an Indian shaman transformed into a hairy demon? Some creature from our own dark dreams? Perhaps some mutation from one of Rubel's experiments in breeding? Whatever it is, recent years have produced no fresh sightings of the Billiwack monster. Perhaps it has moved on, seeking less civilized environs.

What beck'ning ghost, along the moonlight shade,
Invites my steps, and points to yonder glade?
--Alexander Pope
**Elegy to the Memory of
an Unfortuate Lady**

The Haunted Inn

As I drove down the small, one-lane road, I felt I had somehow been transported back in time to the era of hard-riding cattlemen and six-gun justice. Before me loomed a large wooden building that seemed to belong on the set of a Western movie.

I parked my car on that warm July afternoon in front of the Stagecoach Inn on Ventu Park Road in Newbury Park. Today the large building is a museum open to the public. But, long ago, it was the only public house in the Conejo Valley. I mounted the wooden porch and looked over the trees and hills surrounding the Inn. It was hard to believe that a busy freeway was less than a mile away.

I had driven to the Stagecoach Inn not to absorb the historical atmosphere but to seek a ghost. The phantom of the Stagecoach Inn has been documented in several books on famous haunted sites. I waited for the rest of my class in Ghost Hunting to arrive. I had decided that the Stagecoach Inn would be a perfect field trip for my would-be ghost seekers. One by one the cars arrived. The docents at the museum were very helpful in organizing a tour of the building.

The Inn is now a historical landmark and is a replica of the original structure built in 1876. Originally it was known as the Grand Union Hotel and was opened to serve as a stage stop. Since then it has served as a hotel, church, school, military academy, tea room and gift shop. The ghost dates from an earlier period when the building was used as a hotel.

Stories of the haunting of the Inn reached the famed parapsychologist, Hans Holzer, who asked for and received permission to visit the Inn. He brought with him the celebrated medium, Sybil Leek. The late Dr. Cyril W. Anderson, the director of the museum, wrote:

> She reported that there was nothing on the first floor, but that there was a strong disturbance on the second floor. She had received a message from a Pierre Duvon, a mountain man who had come to the Inn for a night's stay in 1885 but had been murdered there while asleep. She described him as a bearded, stocky man about thirty-five years old. She questioned me, but I knew of no corroborating evidence.

A month after the ghost hunt and after a newspaper story about the ghost of Pierre had been published, a man came to Dr. Anderson with a pair of leather chaps with a pistol holster. He said that his father had given them to him with the story that they belonged to the fellow who was murdered in the Inn. The chaps were added to the collection of the museum.

The old Inn was in the path of an expansion of the freeway. To save the historic structure, the building had to be moved. Dr. Anderson recalled a strange event that happened.

> While the Inn was being prepared for moving from the freeway, I went to the site and talked with a workman on the job. He told me that a 'screwy' thing had happened to him that morning while he was on the ground below seeing to placing rollers under it (the house). A big length of two-by-four came hurtling out of an open second floor window and 'damned near brained me.' He was so angry that he rushed up the stairs to see who was so careless. But, he found no one there!

A fire destroyed the historic Inn in 1970, but even this destruction was not without its paranormal implications. One of those present took photographs of the blaze. When these pictures were examined, it was found that a face of a whiskered man was seen in three of the exposures. Could it have been the face of Pierre?

The docents gave us a good deal of the history of the Stagecoach Inn and then escorted me and my students up the narrow staircase to the second floor.

When I walked into the "haunted room" I sensed something, a vibration or somber feeling. I had experienced nothing like it elsewhere in the building. I asked if this was the infamous room where Pierre is believed to have been murdered. I had never been to the place before and there was no indication that this room was the haunted chamber. When I asked, the docent shook her head and said no. But I knew my feelings were not in error. A check with the head of the museum proved my impression was correct. Others in our group also felt a disturbance in the room. Several of my students felt a cold spot near the stairs.

I have no explanation of how I knew that particular room was the legendary haunted room. I must have been directed by some psychic force.

The Haunted Inn

The Stagecoach Inn Museum is open today to the public and I recommend it to anyone interested in the early history of Ventura County. It is well worth a visit. Perhaps you may encounter the icy presence of the ghost named Pierre.

> Ghost: The outward visible manifestation of an inward fear."
>
> --Ambrose Bierce,
> **Devil's Dictionary**

Why do they whistle so loud, when they walk
    past the graveyard late at night?
Why do they look behind them when they
    reach the gate?
Why do they have any gate? Why don't
    they **go through the wall?**
But why, O why do they make that horrible
    whistling sound?

GO AWAY, LIVE PEOPLE, STOP HAUNTING THE DEAD!

Kenneth Fearing
Thirteen O'clock

Georges
The Dramatic Ghost Of The Conejo Players

For years stories have been reported of a ghost in the Conejo Playhouse on South Moorpark Road in Thousand Oaks. This phantom was referred to as "Alfred" by the members of the dramatic group. It is said that this spirit likes musicals. One evening, during a musical production, he was heard loudly walking up and down. After the performance, when they were cleaning up the theater, a napkin was found, dropped by one of the audience, marked with the name "Alfred." The cast and crew gave that name to the phenomenon.

The ghost seems to be a friendly spirit whose presence is never looked upon with dread. Several times items were moved about or temporarily lost. These events were blamed on Alfred. Some of the group even started to refer to the ghost by a second name, "George." One member of the crew told of being followed home by the phantom!

The ghost in the playhouse was even recorded in Hans Holzer's book, **Ghosts of the Golden West.** I had heard these tales for years but never had the time or resources to conduct an investigation. While teaching an advanced course in Ghost Hunting, I planned a series of field trips to reportedly haunted sites. One trip was to a well-documented historic home in Calabasas, but I failed to receive permission to tour the home with my class. Needing a place to visit in the Conejo Valley, I remembered the old stories of the Conejo Playhouse and gave those in charge a call.

They were extremely helpful and agreed to let my class visit the playhouse on a Saturday afternoon. Mrs. P_____ felt a presence the moment we entered the modern building. During the entire tour of the building she felt watched by the ghost. I felt uneasy too, as if unseen eyes were upon me. Several others in the class reported feelings like this.

The Conejo players were in the middle of a performance of the musical, "Pippin," and the stage was set in the simple style of that play. The theater was properly charged with psychic energy; traces of emotion left by so many actors giving their all to so many demanding parts. Still, I began to sense that there might be something else in the building besides psychic residue. As I mounted to the stage my attention was drawn to the wings. One of my students had located a spot that seemed disturbed.

Georges

Mrs. P_____ also felt a man's presence and asked if his name was Alfred. She was mentally informed "My name is not Alfred!" She then reinquired if his name was George. His answer was "Try an 'S'." So, perhaps the specter is named Georges or George S.

I walked into the dressing rooms and felt something in the men's room--as if I were being watched. The ladies' room seemed empty of this feeling. We walked back across the theater to the lighting booth, where some of the members of the playhouse have felt a presence. It did indeed seem charged.

Above the playhouse is a small crawlspace that can be reached via a ladder. From this cramped location some of the spotlights are operated. One section seemed strangely cold. It was a good spot to watch the stage. If there was a ghost who wanted to see the show, this spot would be the best place from which to see it.

Mrs. P_____ had formed a very strong link with the ghost known as Georges, so strong that she could even describe him. She felt that he may have been English or French and a very proper gentleman. This might explain why he is not felt in the ladies dressing room. A drawing of George's face was made from Mrs. P_____'s physical description of him.

The ghost likes to see a show well done and, when he sees shoddy work, he makes his displeasure known with loud footsteps and other disturbances. It seems the Conejo Playhouse has a built-in critic.

> Ghosts do fear no laws
> Nor do they care for popular applause.
> > Anon. (16th century)

The Phantom Committee of the Conejo

The first psychic event I can recall experiencing happened twenty-five years ago. We were living in Thousand Oaks at the time. This was before the massive expansion of the freeway which changed forever the small town atmosphere of the community. It was this mysterious event that may have directed me toward my interest in the paranormal.

We lived on a small hill at that time, without close neighbors, where the sound of people talking late at night was so odd that I rose from my bed to examine the cause. I first believed that guests had arrived late or that a radio or television set had been accidentally left on. The voices were mingled together as if a group of people were talking at the same time. I looked out the windows and in the bright full moonlight I could see that no group of individuals congregated outside. I checked the rest of the house--no one else was awake, the T.V. and radio were off.

Curious, and armed with a powerful lamp, I walked outside seeking the source of the phenomenon. At this point, I thought there must be a logical explanation for the sounds. However, I discovered no parties, no winds, nothing to cause the odd manifestation. I sensed it was not of this world and I quickly returned to my bed.

The next morning I tried to explain away my experience as a dream or perhaps some sound produced by birds or insects. But the strange voices returned, only on this occasion three members of my family heard them as well. The voices were not my imagination!

We called the phenomenon 'the ghostly committee.' It was heard perhaps twelve times during our stay in Thousand Oaks. Every member of our family heard the mysterious voices. It never happened at a set time. Perhaps months would pass between occurrences. Sometimes it would last five or ten minutes, other times an hour or more. Soon the ghostly committee became one of our family's institutions.

One evening when I was in the eighth grade, I invited a close friend over to spend the night. My friend Colin did not believe in the supernatural and often laughed at those who were superstitious. But, before the evening was over, he had changed his opinion dramatically.

It was that night that the committee chose to make itself manifest. It was approximately 12:30 at night when the voices started. We had been talking and laughing for hours and had just settled down to bed. "What's that?" he asked. "Oh, just the ghostly committee," I answered, telling him about the phenomenon. I had heard it so often that it seemed commonplace. At first he believed I was joking and that the voices were some type of elaborate hoax. I told him to check for himself if he did not believe me. I even handed him a flashlight. "Look all you want, there is nothing there."

As soon as he stepped outside, the voices stopped. He spent almost twenty minutes looking before returning to bed, frustrated. Just as he turned out the lights, the eerie voices started once more. Quickly he leaped out of bed, seized the flashlight and bounded out the door. I laughed a little at his discomfort.

When Colin returned five minutes later, the voices had stopped. Again when the lights went out the committee began. My school friend searched for the source of the sounds, but again was frustrated. He did not sleep well that night. The voices stopped about 3:00 a.m.

What was the ghostly committee? I do not know. No previous structure had been built on that site. There was no history of this hill being used for meetings. No legend named the spot as a place where a murder or lynching had taken place. The voices seemed to be speaking English. A few individual words were occasionally made out, such as, "have," "about," and "for." Names and complete sentences were never discerned, only tantalizing tidbits.

My mother, who was highly interested in the supernatural, believed the voices belonged to guardian spirits who were discussing how best to help our family. We were never afraid of the mysterious sounds so they were interpreted as a good omen. Years later I learned that others in the Conejo Valley had also heard the strange voices. Perhaps the committee watched more than one Conejo family.

Poltergeist at Lake Sherwood

A large picturesque home in the exclusive Lake Sherwood area of the Conejo Vally in Ventura County was the scene of a classic polterqeist haunting. The family first heard raps and footsteps and then one morning found every faucet in the house turned on. Each morning the furniture in the home was moved by unseen hands. The doors were locked and checked, yet each morning the tables and chairs were moved. Vases on the mantle of the fireplace were discovered on the floor arranged in a line on the rug.

For weeks the manifestations plagued the family. At last they became so distracted that they did not pick up their option to purchase the house and moved away in fear and panic. Another family dwells in the hous today, but have not complained of ghosts. This is typical of polterqeists. They seem to haunt people rather than places. In some cases the polterqeist follows the fleeing families to other locations. In the vast majority of cases, however, polterqeists seem to leave after only a few weeks as unexpectedly as they arrived.

Westlake's Disappearing Hitchhiker

In June of 1980 a friend related this curious story to me. A friend of hers was near the Westlake onramp to the 101 freeway. There she saw an old man hitchhiking. Although she never picks up hitchhikers, for some reason she stopped and picked this one up. The old man seemed confused and disoriented. She pulled onto the freeway with her strange passenger. At last the hitchhiker cried out, "Christ is coming, Christ is coming!"

The driver looked at him, then glanced at the road, then looked again at the old man. He had vanished! Badly shaken, the woman pulled over to the side of the highway. Eventually a policeman pulled over to help, asking if anything was wrong. She told him her story and was surprised when the officer replied, "You're the fourth one this has happened to today."

The same tale has been reported in other states. Recently in a small town in Arkansas a hitchhiker who vanished was seen by several reliable witnesses. His message was the same; "Christ is coming, Christ is coming!" Perhaps it is the ghost of a minister or missionary on one long continuation of his life's work.

I do not feel myself authorized to reject all ghost stories; from however improbable one taken alone might appear, the mass of them taken together command some credence.

Immanuel Kant

Haunted Ghost Town of Las Llajas Canyon

Deep in Las Llajas Canyon, near Santa Susana, stand the crumbling ruins of a ghost town known as Pisgah Grande. The hollow brick buildings once teemed with life and hope. They stand now windswept and ghost ridden.

Pisgah Grande was built as a Pentecostal Christian Commune, founded by Dr. Finis E. Yoakum to help the less fortunate. The buildings were raised to serve as a rehabilitation center in the early years of the twentieth century, before government welfare agencies were formed to fill that need. The commune flourished from 1914 to 1921. Bricks made on the site were used to construct kitchens, dining rooms, sleeping quarters, a school, homes and a post office. High above the small community the faithful built a brick tower where members set up a twenty-four hour prayer vigil, worshipping God in shifts. Many joined the commune from the skid rows of Los Angeles, turning away from lives of crime to move to the remote town in the hills. One of Dr. Yoakum's early converts at Pisgah Grande was Billy Stiles, who in his youth had ridden with the Jesse James gang. He would entertain the other members by telling of train robberies and bank holdups committed before his conversion and renunciation of the outlaw life.

The religious sect slowly fell apart after the death of its founder in 1920. The brick buildings so laboriously raised were abandoned. Weeds took over the cultivated fields and covered the graves of the small cemetery.

But the ruins are not uninhabited. Many have seen strange things in the deserted town. Others report sounds of voices and loud thumps and knocks. Several visitors claim to have seen a floating white light at the town. They describe it as a glowing square of light moving among the buildings and trees. Could this be the ghost of Dr. Yoakum, whose dream dissolved after his death? Or perhaps it is the troubled specter of one of those buried at Pisgah Grande, whose grave was left untended.

Today, no one lives within at the complex of buildings. Those who have attempted to stay at night tell of feelings of being watched and refuse to spend another sleepless night on the site. Many believe it is the most haunted place in all of Ventura County.

A note of warning to would-be ghost hunters: the ghost town is on private property and armed watchmen are employed to keep out trespassers. Permission must be obtained before venturing into the site. A sign on the private road to the town reads: "No trespass, Have gun will shoot."

Heed the sign well. Pisgah Grande needs no more ghosts to mar its peace.

The Fillmore Lady

Highway 126, a two-lane road, winds from Santa Paula to Castaic Junction and has claimed many lives. At night the twisting ribbon of pavement is a dark and treacherous thoroughfare. Besides the hazards that are common to every well-used county road, this highway also includes the ghost of the White Lady.

I interviewed a man who had encountered this troublesome spirit on the road late at night. Mr. David S_____, who works for a small business in Santa Paula, was returning to his parents' house. David is a dark-haired man in his late twenties with a college degree. He is not one to be shaken by normal events, but this occurrence left him troubled. He was driving on 126 near Fillmore, having just crossed the Sespe, when he saw what he thought was a piece of white paper blowing in the wind. As he raced closer, he saw it was a woman in white hitchhiking alongside the road. She seemed to shine with a soft white light, even though it was a dark, moonless night.

"It gave me the creeps!" he added. He did not pause to slow down but, without looking at her, he raced past. Curiosity got the better of him and he glanced back into his rear-view mirror to see if he had just imagined he had seen a ghostly figure by the side of the road. To his horror he saw the White Lady in his back seat looking at him. Her eyes were like glowing stars. She had long black hair and a deathly white light about her. Almost losing control of his car, he looked into the back seat. It was empty! "I would have jumped right out of the car if I had seen it in the back seat." Even at that, he almost drove off the road into an orchard.

David doesn't drive the road at night now--at least, not alone. The white lady has been seen off and on around Fillmore. Legend states it is the spirit of a girl killed by a train as she wandered the railroad tracks at night. The whitish spirit is seen as a vague form on summer nights. Usually she is reported near the railroad tracks where she met her tragic end. So, when you drive 126 at night, do not be surprised if you see the white lady--and try not to lose control.

From Ghoulies and Ghosties and long-leggety Beasties
And things that Go Bump in the Night
Good Lord, Deliver Us!

Scottish prayer

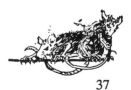

The Curse of the Lost Padres' Mine

Somewhere deep in the remote regions of Ventura County a long-unused tunnel may lead into a fantastic vein of gold. The mine may be dangerous now to those who would tap its wealth, but the lure of the Lost Padres' Mine still draws dozens of men each year to seek Ventura County's El Dorado.

Legend holds that the mine was operated by the Franciscan padres from Mission San Buenaventura. Indian converts, under the guidance of the padres, worked the mine, digging deeper and deeper into the mountain, hauling out rich gold ore. It is claimed that the missionaries built a small adobe chapel near the entrance of the mine so that the Indians could worship without leaving the area. The ore was refined by primitive means and taken by mules down the Santa Clara River valley to the Mission, where it was placed aboard galleons for shipment to Mexico and Spain.

In the 1830s the mission lands were divided into parcels in a painful process called secularization. Many of the padres were ordered back to Spain. Not wanting to share the rich mine with others, they closed down the operation, demolished the chapel and concealed the entrance of the shaft. In a dramatic gesture, the monks gathered the Indian workers and told them that a terrible curse rested upon the mine and on anyone who revealed its location. Those who did would be struck down by the wrath of an angry God. The fearful Indians believed the curse and never betrayed the secret of the mine's location.

There are many tales of lost bonanzas in California. Stories abound about lost gold or silver mines at the twenty-one Spanish missions of California. The Chumash Indians tell about one of their people who defied the curse and sought to locate the lost gold mine operated by the padres. The stories say this mine was located somewhere near Mount Raphael in Santa Barbara County. The greedy Indian managed to find the concealed shaft but, upon entering, he was struck dead by the curse. The Chumash say his moaning spirit still guards the location, ready to enforce the stringent curse. The Indians avoid the area, believing a terrible fate will fall upon any who stray too near the old tunnel.

Another tale is related that an aged Indian in the 1880s agreed to lead greedy Americans to the site of a mine worked by the Mission San Buenaventura. The desperation and poverty of the Indian overcame his fear of the awful curse. He had worked in the mine as a young man and knew of its location near the headwaters of Piru Creek.

The expedition of treasure-seekers had not ridden far out of Santa Paula when the aged Indian guide fell from his horse screaming. It was some time before the Indian was able to tell them that he had been struck blind! The curse had reached out from the mine to strike down those who would betray the location of the Lost Padres' gold!

There is some basis of fact for the existence of a lost mine. In 1842 gold was discovered in Placerita Canyon near Piru. It was discovered by a vaquero named Francisco Lopez while digging for wild onions for his lunch. He recognized the tiny flakes of gold clinging to the roots of the onions. This discovery sparked a small gold rush of Mexican miners who came north out of Sonora to exploit the strike. They soon depleted the gold in both Francisquito and Placerita Canyons and returned to Mexico, ignorant of the huge gold fields at the foot of the Sierras that sparked the great California gold rush of 1849.

Skeptics believe that tales of lost mines are just oral traditions of the 1842 gold strike in Ventura County. But what of the terrible curse? In 1887 a town named Lexington was formed near the headwaters of Piru and Lockwood Creeks; the reputed site of the Lost Padres' Mine. The town was laid out and several lots sold, but after only a few weeks it was gone, a ghost town before it had even begun. Perhaps Lexington was another victim of the curse?

Legends say the mine entrance is marked by two large trees. If it exists at all, it would be a narrow hole in the side of a mountain, leading to a bonanza of untapped gold. But, for those who seek this wealth, beware of the terrible curse that strikes all who seek the Lost Padres' Mine.

Ghosts of Fort Tejon

Our group met in Ventura to begin a journey that would take us eighty miles away and 130 years back in time. Twelve of us, with packed lunches, tape recorders, cameras and pads of paper, began our journey seeking the truth behind the legends of a ghost seen at the old site of Fort Tejon. The fort, or I should say that small part of the fort that is restored, is a California state historic park. It stands as a museum dedicated to the period of American occupation of California.

The old outpost is located in Grapevine Canyon on Highway 99, seventy-seven miles north of Los Angeles, near the small town of Lebec. The fort was established by the United States Army on August 10, 1854, and became the headquarters of the First U.S. Dragoons. The Dragoons guarded miners, chased bandits and horse thieves, and served as escorts to Los Angeles and Salt Lake City.

Once over twenty buildings made up the post that was one of the largest settlements in Southern California at the time. The fort was abandoned in 1864 and the land and buildings became part of General Beal's Tejon Rancho. The five-acre historic park was granted to the State by the Tejon Ranch in 1939.

The restored adobe structures show the types of buildings used at the post. Today only three buildings and a small museum remain of the once flourishing military base. The isolation in the mountains makes this park ideal as a place to detect psychometry. The still, crisp mountain air was an unexpected environment for the site of a haunting.

In the northwest corner of the parade ground is the Peter Le Beck oak. The oak tree was discovered in 1853 to have a mysterious inscription carved deep into the bark:

"Peter Le Beck, killed by a X bear,
Oct. 17th 1837"

It is believed that a French trapper was slain on that site, but who he was or who buried him and left the carving remains a compelling mystery. It is reported that an apparition, thought to be the spirit of Le Beck, has been seen at the fort.

The story is told of how, after the military base was established, the good Christian women of the fort caused the soldiers to dig up the bones of the Frenchman from the base of the oak and move them to a proper cemetery, where he was given a Christian service. Peter Le Beck is said to have begun his wanderings then in protest of the desecration of his grave. He was probably not a Christian and was deeply disturbed by such a rite pronounced over his bones. Perhaps he wanders the fort longing for his old grave.

I had heard of this legend from a student several years ago. He told me that tours given by the ranger at the fort always included the ghost of Le Beck as part of the fort's lore. The story sounded like just another tale that became attached to the history of the lonely site. It was classified as another apocryphal legend and, as such, given a low priority in my research on the paranormal. When recently I had the time, I returned to Fort Tejon to look more closely at the tales of Le Beck's ghost.

The group of investigators met near the small museum at the fort and split up to begin the individual part of the ghost hunt. After forty-five minutes we regathered at the museum and had lunch. We ate our meal by a rushing stream. After we ate, I gave a short lecture on the history of the site, then we told what each of us felt.

A variety of psychic impressions were felt at the lonely site. One person felt a great disturbance near several large oak trees. She felt that once a hanging had taken place there. She sensed a name, "Chief Black Bear." Perhaps a local Indian was put to death under that very tree. Another felt a stabbing pain strike between the shoulder blades. She felt a murder or grievous assault had taken place before the small adobe building designated as the orderlies' quarters. The dilapidated structure seemed to be the center of several strong vibrations. Another felt nauseous. Others felt great anger and frustration. Still another saw a vision of a dirty, weathered wagon inside the building--where it was put to keep it out of the elements, as in a garage or carriage house. Most felt ill at ease near the building.

Near the orderlies' quarters stands the two-storied officers' quarters. Several felt strange vibrations from this adobe structure. It was used as a farm house after the abandonment of the fort. Because it was maintained, it has survived, while almost all of the adobe buildings have returned to the soil. This modest house seemed charged with overlapping feelings. Some felt a terrifying force in the basement. Others detected the sound of several women singing and talking. The house had once been a place of intense activity. The upper floors seemed to be charged also, but the feeling there was sadness--the people who had lived there were very unhappy. The wives of those frontier officers were not overjoyed to live at such a lonely outpost. Many missed the comforts of the older established bases in the East.

The long barracks is only a reconstruction of the original structure. It did not have any psychic impressions that were detectable by our group. The site of the mess hall behind the barracks did hold some traces. One member felt it was "like a Boy Scout camp," with the noises of hungry men. The site of the hospital across the parade grounds seemed to be charged with energy. Most hospitals are haunted, so it did not seem inconsistent that strong traces of emotion should remain on that site. One of our company felt an entrance in one section. The hospital was built near the haunted oak tree, leading us to speculate that the ghost seen at the old fort is not the French trapper but the spirit of one of the Dragoons who died in the hospital.

Beyond the orderlies' quarters is a grave--a monument to one of the men who died at the fort. Those who visited the grave site felt nothing there. When the forest ranger at the park was questioned about the grave, he said that the bodies of the dead were dug up when the base was abandoned in 1864. That would explain why the grave felt so empty. Perhaps the ghost seen was one of those who was buried and left behind in the graveyard. The ranger said he had never seen or heard a thing at the fort but others who have visited the place have reported feeling odd and seeing things. One ranger who worked there years ago did see things and refused to stay at the fort after dark by himself. Whatever haunts the old establishment, it shall wander the lonely, foreboding buildings of the fort until released by time or deed.

Apparition of La Llorona—The Crier

She looked at me across the table, her dark eyes flashing, and said, "Don't mess with her! She kills people!" I had met with Miss R_____ and Miss C_____ on a warm April afternoon in the coffee shop of Ventura College. In such a bright and cheerful place it is difficult to imagine the full horror of the events these two had witnessed. They were business students at the college, both of Mexican-American descent, and raised in the traditions of their heritage. That heritage includes the chilling specter of La Llorona.

La Llorona in Spanish means "the crier." Legend says she was an evil woman who was unfaithful to her husband in Old Mexico. She drowned her three children because they came between her and a lover. For her awful crime she was cursed by God to wander the earth seeking her lost children. If she finds any stray children at night, she will kill them and take their souls. La Llorona is known by her terrible cry, said to sound like a mixture of a crying child and a siren.

Miss R_____ sipped on her soft drink and started to relate her experience as I tried to keep up with the narrative with pad and pen. "We were living in Oxnard at that time," Miss R_____ began. "I guess I was about fourteen. We were living in a large house and I had a small bedroom toward the back. I woke up late at night right out of a sound sleep. It was like I heard something. Like maybe a fire engine. It was really dark and I can remember I was not afraid, at least not yet."

"I got up to go to the bathroom down the hall. There was no light in the hallway and, as I got up, I saw someone at the end of the hall in front of the bathroom door. It seemed to glow all over as if it had a halo around it. It was a lady in a long black dress. The dress shined like silk. She had dark hair--but no face!" Miss R_____ stared at me with a look of deep conviction. I could sense this was no fabrication. "I could feel evil coming out of the lady. I just stood there, not knowing what to do. Then she started to slowly glide towards me. It was maybe eighteen feet away. It did not walk, but slid towards me. I was too scared to scream. I ran back to my room and slammed the door shut, and I started to pray. I've never prayed so hard in all my life." The terrifying specter did not bother her again, nor has she seen the awful dark lady since.

Miss C_____ had also seen the apparition. "Lots of people

have seen 'the lady,'" she said. "My sister saw her once floating in the air. If you say her name the lady will come for you. It is no joke. She will come to your window at night and look in at you." I asked her what she had seen.

College students were eating and talking in the coffee shop, but our round table seemed surrounded by an eerie stillness, almost as if we were in a sound-proof bubble.

"I was seventeen. I had had a fight with my mother. I was in my room, combing my hair. I guess it was about 11:30 at night and I had my window shade open behind me. I looked in the mirror and, over my shoulder, I could see my open window. As I was combing my hair, I felt a cold chill like a gust of wind. I looked in my mirror and saw the lady looking in at me from the window. She had long black hair and a white space where her face should have been. I turned around and she was still there, just looking at me. It lasted maybe a minute, maybe less. It was horrible."

The legend of La Llorona may go as far back as Aztec mythology. Some say that the tale was brought up from Mexico by the first settlers to our state. Others believe the ghost simply followed them north. The incidents reported by the two college students are not unique. La Llorona has been seen many times in the county, usually near the Santa Clara River.

Some say that the stories are told by mothers to frighten their children into behaving--a sort of mexican Boogie Man. This theory is rebuked by those who have seen the terrible apparition of La Llorona.

> But why do I talk of Death?
> That Phantom of grisly bone,
> I hardly fear its terrible shape,
> It seems so like my own.
> > Thomas Hood

"Something is Watching Us!"

It was my first semester teaching a class called "Ghosts and Hauntings" when I was informed of the haunted bank in Oxnard. The phantom had persistently appeared in the building on a certain day of the week with such regularity that the tellers were gripped by fear. Several had terminated their employment because of the ghostly lady. Raps were heard, strange footsteps were manifest, screams echoed in the building as well as the unnerving tinkling of invisible bells.

Oddly enough, the haunted bank is a modern structure without a history of any sort of tragedy. A new building, it reflects the current style of color and light, pleasant and comfortable. It is not the somber and solid environment of banks constructed years ago. By all rights such a relaxed, color-coordinated place of business should not be haunted.

I interviewed several of the tellers. The fear in their eyes and the conviction of their tone left little doubt in my mind that something sinister dwelled within the bank. It was described as a vague figure without features, just a human form. Instinctively they felt it was a woman. The apparition appeared to be nine feet tall and moved with a gliding motion over the floor. It moved with alarming speed.

Once the phantom materialized behind a railing next to the counter of the bank. The specter did not pass through the rail but simply rose over the obstacle and floated on. The ghostly lady seems to be most active in the afternoon hours just before closing time.

The tellers also reported hearing loud thumps just before closing. It sounds "like someone banging on a hollow log." Other times loud footsteps are heard, like someone walking on a hardwood floor. Yet all the floors in the bank are carpeted! The tellers sensed that "something is watching us!"

With a group of students from my class, I investigated the bank. The sounds could not have originated from other buildings and reflection did not seem to be responsible for the whitish apparition. The floor did not seem capable of producing sounds of footsteps. The carpet was thick enough to muffle even the stamping of a boot. Some of the air vents on the side of the building were pointed out by one of the student investigators as a source for the rapping. A cover on the vent could rattle. Although the interior of the bank is attractively decorated and

47

sunny, I could feel an underlying tension.

I asked if I could see the upper floor of the bank. It is mostly office space and had been the site of several psychic events. As I mounted the carpeted staircase my heart began to beat faster. I too could feel that unseen eyes were watching me. I realized at once that the disturbance at the bank was focused on the second floor.

When I entered one of the rooms on the upper floor I felt a presence. My scalp started to tingle as I slowly walked forward in the semi-darkness. I encountered what felt like a wall of vibration. It was a tingling sensation that could only be described as pins and needles. We left the bank after obtaining permission to come again the next week.

Much of ghost hunting is not wandering around musty haunted houses. Much of it entails research in local libraries and records offices. This necessary but often dull task I delegated to my student investigators. As I suspected, one of my students discovered that a two-story wooden home had once occupied the very location of the bank. I had guessed as much when we were informed that the phantom appeared to be nine feet tall. As specters try to duplicate life as much as possible, a nine-foot ghost would be unlikely unless there was a good reason.

The only explanation seemed that the apparition was walking upon the floor of a house that was no longer present. The floor of the house must have been three or four feet higher than the cement floor of the bank. This psychic floor would also explain the odd footsteps. They could be products of a spectral hardwood floor.

It was theorized that a spectral two-storied farm house was superimposed upon the modern bank. This would explain the "wall of vibration" I had felt on the second floor. I may have been walking through a spirit wall into the former location of a room that had witnessed some awful tragedy.

The next week our group arrived at the bank with the research we had uncovered. It was at this visit that we learned that one of the tellers had interviewed her grandmother. A long time resident of Ventura County, she had spent most of her life living not far from the bank. She remembered that a woman had been "beaten to death" by her husband approximately on that site many decades ago.

We decided that research and an on-site investigation could add little to what we knew of the bank. The next step was to hold a seance to see if new information could be gained about the ghostly lady. After receiving permission from the bank personnel to use a room on the second floor, we proceeded with our plans for this experiment in spirit communication.

I decided that a simple Ouija board might be the most efficient tool for our sitting. [A word of warning should be included at this point. Ouija boards are not toys and should be used under controlled supervision. Parapsychologists warn against prolonged use of the board. Case studies show that prolonged use can form serious psychological dependency. I advise anyone who has experienced anything <u>negative</u> on a Ouija board to <u>cease using the instrument at once!</u>]

The group was divided in half with each session made up of different people. The first seance was made up of five members with a reporter from a newspaper observing. There seemed to be a distinct coldness in the room as we asked if the ghost was indeed a woman. The board moved to "yes." The air was heavy as we watched the glass we were using as a planchet move slowly over the board. We took turns asking questions, taking detailed notes of our responses.

Q) Are you troubled?
A) Yes.
Q) Is there something we can do for you?
A) Death. Murder.
Q) You were murdered?
A) Yes.
Q) What kind of weapon killed you?
A) Chain.
Q) Strangled with a chain?
A) Yes.
Q) Do you know the name of your murderer?
A) Yes
Q) Can you give us that name?
A) No.
Q) Can God help you?
A) <u>Luz</u> (Spanish for light).

Over and over again the words "death" and murder" came. The date 1917 also was consistent. The communication also went on to state that the murderer had never been brought to justice. The room came alive with tense expectation at this question:
Q) Will you manifest yourself today?
A) Yes.

We waited, attentive to every sound and movement, but nothing supernatural occurred. The first sitting ended when no more information could be gathered from the board.

We later learned that one of the tellers who had not been present during the Ouija board experiment saw "something white" watching her from a second floor window as she left for the day!

A second seance was held a week later. I did not take an active part in this meeting, and those who worked the Ouija board had not been present at the first session. They were not privy to what had transpired before. The planchet moved slowly at first, then it seemed to gain strength forming the responses to our questions.

Q) What is your first name?
A) Agatha.
Q) Were you killed by a man?
A) No.
Q) What instrument was used to kill you?
A) Chain.
Q) Would you give your murderer's first name?
A) Helena.
Q) Were you related to Helena?
A) No.
Q) Was Helena your husband's mistress?
A) Yes.
Q) What year did this murder take place?
A) 1917.
Q) Are there any other spirits here besides you, Agatha?
A) Sometimes.
Q) Why are you here? Why do you haunt?
A) No home.
Q) Do you seek something here?
A) Revenge.
Q) On whom do you wish to have revenge?
A) Her.
Q) Is her spirit here?
A) Yes.
Q) Are there two spirits here?
A) Yes.

The hate between Agatha and the murderous Helena had caused the disturbances at the bank. Both spirits inhabited the bank and were responsible for the sounds and apparitions. The seance ended with little new information on the haunting, but everyone walked away drained of energy. We were left with several odd facts. Both sessions mentioned a chain as a murder weapon and the date 1917. Yet both groups had been separated.

As I was leaving the bank that last time a rather curious incident took place. I draw no conclusion from it, but I record it here as a postscript to our seance. I was carrying the Ouija board out to my car when the inverted glass we had been using as a planchet flew from my hand and shattered against the pavement.

In all fairness, I must add that the Ouija board is an unreliable tool. Records do not show people with those names living near the site of the bank, nor is there any report of a murder there. Still, in the weeks following the experiment, the bank calmed down. Fewer and fewer encounters with the ghost were reported. Perhaps our simple seance brought peace to the troubled spirit.

Next time you go to a bank in Oxnard, and I am not at liberty to disclose which one, and you see a flash out of the corner of your eye, it might not be a trick of your optic nerve. You may have had a glimpse of "Agatha" or "Helena."

Silver Strand Haunting

The Silver Strand area, adjacent to the Channel Islands Harbor, is a peaceful beach front community that traces its roots to the days long ago when silent films, including the **Sheik**, were shot there in the 1920s. Many of the streets are narrow and swept by sand. Perhaps the streets and faded street markers are the cause of my getting lost.

I had been called in to investigate the haunting of one of the beach front cottages in Silver Strand. I had brought with me for this investigation a gifted psychic. I had not told her about the disturbances in the house, yet she sensed something as we drew near an old board fence. "This is the house, it's here, it is so sad." Checking my notes, the psychic was correct--this humble, rather ramshackle structure was our destination.

The young owner was waiting for us. She had phoned after encountering something in her house--something she could not understand. As she greeted us, I asked her not to tell about the haunting; so that the psychic could sense what was in the house.

The lady was silent. I turned on the tape recorder and followed the psychic as she slowly moved from room to room in the well-furnished cottage. The psychic could detect many personal things about the new owner but nothing psychic--no specters. After writing up our limited findings in the cottage we progressed into the adjoining garage. As soon as we entered the dank building we were greeted by an icy cold; a cold that seemed to have no source yet it chilled to the bone. The garage had been converted into a small apartment which contained a small kitchen and bathroom with a shower. One wall was a large window that suggested an artist's studio. Dust and mildew told of a long period of disuse.

The psychic began to tremble. "He is here." She whispered, "There is a presence." I could feel the cold and the intense depression, yet could see nothing. The psychic now began to stare toward the shower area in the converted garage. "I can see him--he is angry," she said. "He wants to know who we are and why we have come here." I instructed the psychic to ask him his name. She said, "Jim. He is coming towards us!" she said. The "sensitive" began to tremble and shake. Her expression changed and her voice dropped lower. "Who are you?" she croaked.

Surprised, I asked who she was. "I live here." I could sense that the spirit in the garage had entered into the psychic. I began to ask questions and learned a terrible story. The young man had lived in the garage years ago. He had taken drugs at a party and his girl friend, Susan, had left for some reason. He had waited for her when he overdosed and died--he waits still.

I told the spirit that he was no longer alive; that he should move on to the next plane of existence. "No," he yelled, "No, I am not dead! You are dead." At that the large window began to rattle and shake as if an earthquake was commencing.

"No," the psychic screamed. "No, I am still alive!" I knew now that the spirit wished to possess the body of the psychic, wished to use the body to maintain a semblance of life. I seized her arm and told the invading spirit to look for the light. The light that has been reported time and again in cases of near death experiences. "They are coming for me!" shouted the psychic in the deep voice of the spirit.

"Who is coming?" I demanded.

"They glow. They glow like jelly. Their hands are reaching out." I told the spirit called Jim to extend his hand. These were the spirit guides sent to escort the trapped soul to the next level of existence.

"No!" he yelled. "I am afraid." I commanded that the spirit reach out for help. Slowly the psychic reached out her hand toward the window. "Go towards them," I comforted. "Go towards the light." At that moment the psychic trembled and I rushed and held her as she collapsed. When she regained consciousness she could recall nothing of the encounter. But the garage seemed light now and the cold had dissipated.

Later, upon discussing the case, we learned that the owner of the house and her friends had not heard or felt an earthquake or sonic boom. Yet we had distinctly experienced the sound in the garge! What could it have been?

This is only one of several houses where spirits walked without knowing they were dead. Many times there is an explanation for the events experienced in haunted houses, but other times the realm of spirits seems to invade the world of the living.

> Do you ever find yourself talking with
> the dead?... I do.
>
> Abraham Lincoln

Haunted House of Port Hueneme

Port Hueneme is an old town with its share of county haunts. One story told is of a large house where things were moved about by unseen hands. The wooden victorian house was peaceful until the new owner ripped open a room that had been boarded up in the basement. This room was empty, but oddly cold and smelly. From that day on strange things began to happen and the family feared that they had released some invisible agent into their home. Furniture in the kitchen was moved about during the night.

For some time, it was believed that people had broken in and were playing pranks. To catch these people, threads were stretched across doorways and the floors were sprinkled with flour to trap footprints. The "booby traps" were in vain for the furniture was moved, but neither the threads nor the flour were disturbed! One room of the house was always cold and very depressing. Nothing could warm it and no one could sleep peacefully there. Today the house is gone, but the stories remain. Now an ice cream shop stands on the site of the haunted house. Could the ghost still be manifest on that location? Perhaps!

Why should there not be ghosts?
Dr. Carl Jung

The Legend of Hueneme
The Lady of Mugu Rock

The legend dates back hundreds of years and was told over and over again by the Chumash Indians. They believed it to be a true tale. Were it not for recent sightings of a ghostly Indian maiden at Mugu Rock, the tale of Hueneme could be discounted as one of the many folklore stories common to the Native Americans.

The legend tells of a beautiful Indian maiden named Hueneme. She was the daughter of a wise and great chief. She was not only beautiful but kind, joyful, and warm. Everyone loved her including the birds who would land upon her shoulder and sing their sweetest songs to her.

Her beauty was renowned among all branches of the Chumash from the islands to the inland valleys. Many young Indian men came seeking her hand in marriage. Many suitors spoke with Hueneme but they were sent away--still happy to have even seen such a lovely and gentle maiden.

At last one man came to Hueneme's village. A tall and brave man, this one she instantly fell in love with and they were married. They settled into a bliss-filled marriage that was spoken of by all the Indians of the coast.

But Hueneme's new husband had attracted the unwanted attentions of another woman. As the woman saw the joy of the couple, her hate grew and she resolved to destroy the marriage. She went to an old sorcerer and learned the black arts of witchcraft.

After she had mastered these wicked skills, the witch woman journeyed to the village where Hueneme and her husband lived. When she once again saw Hueneme's great beauty, goodness, and happiness, the evil woman grew dark with envy and hate. The witch woman carefully began to work her foul magic. She burned black feathers and chanted a weird song. She cast her spell upon Hueneme's husband. "You have beauty, Hueneme," she sang, "and you have goodness, but you cannot also have love. This I will take from you!" With spells she caused the husband to be blinded to his wife's beauty and kindness. With magic she caused his love to become hate. And so, when the young man looked upon his wife, he saw not her but another. His eyes were only open for the witch woman. She caused him to love her and come away to her valley.

With tearful eyes, Hueneme returned to her home and spoke with her wise father. The old chief told her to seek her husband for the witch woman's magic could not blind the man forever. "Love cannot be destroyed by an evil spirit." She trusted her father's words and traveled from village to village, asking all she met if they knew where her husband had gone. A friend told her where the witch woman had taken her husband and she walked to a far valley where the evil woman lived. It was a forbidding valley with few trees and where a great stink issued from the parched earth. It was cursed by the witch woman's wickedness. There she found the man and the witch woman. He did not recognize her face at first, so blinded had he become, but the music of her voice parted the dark veil of the spell and he grew sad at the loss of her kindness and gaiety.

She walked out of the cursed valley and her husband followed her, for he realized that there could be no happiness in his life without Hueneme. They walked to Point Mugu where he built a hut for them. They dwelled there together but the happiness they once had was not to be found for the evil spell lingered on. The magic had not been fully lifted from his heart.

As the days passed, Hueneme became filled with despair. She forgot that love cannot be destroyed by curses or spells and that, in time, the evil would depart from the man, and his love for her would be rekindled.

Hueneme moaned in sadness at the edge of the pounding ocean. At last, in despair, she heeded the calling of the cold sea and walked into the beckoning waves. Her husband saw her action and, filled with grief, followed her into the sea. The Chumash believed that the gods changed both of them to stone.

There is a rock off Point Mugu which is thought to be that of the Indian maiden, Hueneme. When the tide is low, half of her body can be seen. Next to this rock is another. This is believed to be her husband. Before the missionaries came to Ventura County, the Indians left bowls of food at Mugu Rock for Hueneme and her husband.

This is the legend of Hueneme. From time to time visitors and campers at Mugu Rock have seen the spirit of an Indian woman near the crashing waves. It is said that it is the sad Hueneme haunting forever the site of her tragic suicide. Odd lights have also been observed by the rock. Legend holds that the supernatural spheres of energy, that linger around the place near the ocean is the evil soul of the witch woman cursed by her magic to wander the rock as punishment for the crime she caused. Perhaps the apparition seen is not Hueneme but the spirit of the hate-filled sorceress.

Ghosts and Hauntings
of
Santa Barbara County

I sit here in this old house and work on foreign affairs, read reports, and work on speeches--all the while listening to the ghosts walk up and down the hallway and even right in here in the study.

Harry Truman
Letter dated June 12, 1945, White House

Ghosts of Santa Barbara County

1. The Haunted Tavern
2. The Haunted Adobe
3. The Ghosts of La Purisima Mission
4. The Black Coach
5. "Las Cruces" Ghost Town
6. The Ghostly Children of Santa Barbara
7. The "Ghost" of Mission Santa Barbara
8. The Black Fisherman
9. The White Lady of Santa Barbara City College
10. The Poltergeist of Hope Ranch
11. The Three Nuns
12. Hector of the Summerland

P.P. 86

Hector, the Ghost of Summerland

So you want to hear about the ghost?" said the young waiter with a flashing smile. "Everyone wants to hear about Hector. He's the ghost of the Big Yellow House." We listened as the young man named Nathan began to tell us of the many encounters the personnel have had with their resident ghost. The stories of this phantom had attracted my attention to the Big Yellow House Restaurant in the small community of Summerland.

Summerland is known for its oil and gas wells in a boom at the end of the nineteenth century, the nude beach patronized years ago by "hippie" flower children, and ghosts. The ghostly connection can be traced to the town's origins in 1883 when it was founded by Mr. H. L. Williams as a center for spiritualism. The religion of spiritualism is based upon the belief that the living can indeed contact the dead by using specially gifted individuals called "mediums." They believe that there are (in classical spiritualism) seven spheres or heavens and the nearest to the earth is called "Summerland." Mr. Williams named his town after one of the spiritualist's heavenly dominions.

The large manor that today houses the restaurant dates its origins to the spiritualist colony. Here seances were held at the turn of the century.

Perhaps with spirits coming and going Hector decided to make this house his permanent home. Converted into a restaurant in 1973, the two storied house became a permanent landmark of Summerland. Soon rumors of ghosts and mysterious events circulated about the house. Because of the tales of The Big Yellow House, I organized a group to determine if it was indeed a haunted site. Our group booked a room and held a dinner at the restaurant. We requested a meeting with some of the employees to learn what kinds of events had been experienced. The manager was not shaken by our request; other groups interested in psychic phenomena had previously gone to the house. One group was a team from the parapsychology laboratory at UCLA.

The dinner was tasty and filling. While sipping coffee a waiter was interviewed. He was a young man named Nathan who had worked for two years at the Big Yellow House. "Yeah, there is a ghost here all right." He began, "lots of people have had things happen to them. Windows go up and down by themselves! Once the manager closed up by himself and when he came into

61

this part of the house all the windows were open. So he closed them again and locked up. The next morning he got in early before anyone else and all the windows were open again. Hector likes to play games with us sometimes. A while back the manager came in early in the morning to find all of the tables stacked one on top of the other all the way to the ceiling. . . and each table was set for dinner, silverware, napkin and table cloth."

I was using a portable tape recorder to get the waiter's story word for word. The rest of our party listened with fascination as Nathan continued his narrative with all the flourishes of a born story teller.

"One of the waitresses years ago came in and found all the dishes in the library room smashed, and another waitress felt something tug on her skirt as she walked on the second floor late one night. "Hector" is here all right but he isn't evil or anything; he just likes to play pranks from time to time."

Nathan went to the door of the room and pointed to the antique doorknob. "This door was closed one evening." He continued, "The manager heard the door rattle and the doorknob shake, but when he checked it there was nobody there. We know who it was; it was 'Hector.'"

I asked why they call the phantom "Hector." The waiter shrugged his shoulders and said that he did not know but that the ghost had always been known by that name.

One member of our group, a medium, agreed to hold a seance in the room to attempt to communicate with "Hector." The young woman realized she had extraordinary abilities when she spoke with her long dead great grandmother at the age of five. Young and attractive, she does not resemble the turbaned bejeweled mediums of fiction. The lights were dimmed and everyone in the room was requested to hold hands in a circle.

The medium began to breathe heavily and go into a deep trance. The room was tense as she inhaled and exhaled going deeper and deeper into a self-induced hypnotic state. In the dim light we waited, not knowing what to expect. Moments passed and at last the medium began to speak in a raspy voice as the room seemed strangely cold. The voice complained of pains in his chest and made rough sounds.

The medium fell forward in a deep sleep. The seance had ended almost as quickly as it had begun. Could she have contacted "Hector"? Was he someone who had died of a heart attack in this house years ago? Is that why he still haunts? She could tell us nothing more from her experience.

The question remains as to who or what walks the halls of the Victorian home that is The Big Yellow House. Could there be a spirit called "Hector" or is it someone or something else?

If on some October night you want to have dinner in an authentic "Haunted House," I recommend The Big Yellow House Restaurant. You might be lucky and see "Hector", the ghost of Summerland.

> People with a certain strength or fixity of purpose may have ghosts of a certain strength and fixity of purpose--most haunting ghosts, you know, must be as one-idea'd as monomaniacs and as obstinate as mules to come back again and again.

--H. G. Wells
The Inexperienced Ghost

The Three Nuns of Ortega Road

Stop the car, she yelled. "It was right there, right by that tree! I am sure. That's where the ghost nuns stood."

I pulled the car onto the dirt siding of the road and braked to a dusty halt. Before I could get out of the car with my tape recorder, she pulled open the door and ran towards the small tree.

Even as I got out of the car I could sense something strange. Maybe it was the colorful sunset that bathed the setting with a purple light.

Maria A_____ was standing near the tree with her arms flayed out in a position that would seem almost ridiculous if one did not know what she had experienced only two weeks before.

"The three nuns stood here." she said. "They had black and white habits and white faces that shined like china." I pressed the record button on my tape recorder and asked her to retell her story.

"My sisters and I were driving down Ortega Road in Montecito, east of Santa Barbara about nine at night. We were visiting her boyfriend. She was returning his jacket. We saw them standing right here looking right at us. They had their arms folded. I can remember their eyes; they sparkled like blue stars... We drove right past them. We all turned and looked back and they were gone." I asked if the others saw them as well as she did. Maria nodded. I asked her to tell the legend of the three nuns she had heard from her aunt.

"Long ago in the mission times there were three nuns who would go out to the Indian villages to treat the sick. There had been a terrible revolt and the nuns were told not to leave the safety of Santa Barbara because of the danger from Indian bands. But trusting to God they decided to go anyway... Here they were captured by wild Indians and tortured."

Maria told how each of the three sisters were subjected to unspeakable mutilations and death at the hands of the natives, yet before each of them lost consciousness they forgave their tormentors for their awful crimes.

From that day on, the three nuns or 'Las Tres Hermanas' have been seen along Ortega Road. I walked near the tree and on the road searching for something that might indicate a rational explanation for the tripartite sighting. I found only a few beer cans and a wine bottle. From the look on Maria's face as she

65

gave her account, I was convinced that something had taken place here. As we drove away she stared at the tree until we turned a corner.

Doing research at the UCSB library on the sighting, I discovered that no holy sisters operated in this area during the mission period, and none of the records tell of any Indian massacres in that location, or of three apparitions.

Folklore does relate similar accounts in Latin America and parts of Southern Europe (Italy and Spain). There are many tales of murdered saints returning to the scenes of their deaths. It is an ancient tradition that can be traced to the origins of the Christian church. Perhaps such stories, or oral traditions, were transplanted to this area from Mexico or Spain--or maybe the nuns chose to follow their countrymen to this new land.

I can still recall the intense look on Maria's face. To her the three nuns were a symbol of her Catholic faith and she was convinced beyond a shadow of a doubt she had indeed encountered 'Las Tres Hermanas.' Who is to say that she didn't?

> Miracles are not contrary to nature; they are only contrary to what we know about nature.
>
> --St. Augustine

The Black Fisherman of Santa Barbara

Dad saw him," she began. "He was baby-sitting for me and saw a tall dark figure with a fisherman's cap."

When she returned her father had been able to say only: "Boy, you got something in this house." Kathi E_____ had been living in the apartment on Ledera Street, Santa Barbara, for less than a year when the odd events began.

"If I had not been a single parent I would have moved away at once, but I stayed another six months." Things got worse until she feared for her safety and sanity.

"It began with rapping and knockings," she continued as I sipped my coffee and took notes of her bizarre encounter with the unknown. "It was a steady pounding on one of the walls between the rooms of my apartment. It was not the pipes. Nothing could account for this racket."

Her friend, Peter, as well as her sister saw the black figure. It was described as tall and jet black. They began to call it "the fisherman" because of the cap it wore. Kathi was unable to determine who it was or why it wished to terrorize her family.

The records of parapsychology are filled with similar accounts of dark figures that frighten people. Many believe they are "evil spirits" doomed to walk for a time on this plane before they can continue on to the next realm. Some believe they are fearful projections from our own minds: terrifying memories of our childhood "boogie men."

Kathi was certain that whatever the vision, it was linked to the site of her apartment. Doing research, she made a startling discovery. In 1851 the common council of Santa Barbara set aside a plot of land on that site for the use of "Protestants and paupers." Most of the inhabitants of the town were Roman Catholic at that time. The graveyard was used for several years before its abandonment. Many who lie buried there may well have been unemployed seamen or fishermen who fell victim to strong drink or violence. Perhaps burial in a pauper's grave desecrated by an apartment building was reason enough for the figure to walk the earth. "It was evil," Kathi exclaimed, "I could just feel it."

We will never know the true nature of the dark phantom of Ladera Street, but if his nocturnal walks persist, perhaps others will encounter his terrifying presence and alert ghost hunters to his existence.

Black Fisherman Of Santa Barbara

Fearing the ghost, Kathi moved from the building before I or my associates could investigate this psychic event.

Who gather round, and wonder at the tale of
horrid apparition, tall and ghastly, that walks
at dead of night or takes his stand
O'er some new-open'd grave; and
(strange to tell!)
E vanishes at crowing of the cock.
--Robert Blair

Hope Ranch Poltergeist

The windshield wipers moved back and forth as I tried to locate a house in the maze-like streets of Santa Barbara's Hope Ranch. The street numbers on the homes were hard to locate because of the lavish landscaping. But Mrs. B_____ was adamant that I drop what I was doing and come at once. There was "something in the house."

I slowed at each cross street until I found the street. I had missed it twice in my wanderings. Finally, I found my destination; a beautiful home set back from the road. A huge picture window looked out from well trimmed shrubs and flowers tended with the meticulousness of a gardener who knew and loved his work.

I parked my car on the street and walked up the broad driveway to the entrance. I did not know what to expect when I pressed the door bell. Chimes sounded and the portal opened to a smiling face of a woman with large glasses and a pink sweater. She looked at me, smiled oddly, and declared, "You're Richard Senate, aren't you?" I nodded and she ushered me out of the rain. Thick carpets, soft furniture, an ancient grandfather clock, and large Japanese prints filled the living room with a sense of subtle affluence. "Would you like coffee?" she asked. I took off my coat and said that a warm cup of coffee would be just the thing on this cold rainy day. I waited in the living room glancing at the Chinese figures on the glass coffee table.

Ghosts do not respect boundaries of class, wealth or culture. They invade where they please. Even though the woman, Mrs. B_____, had been gracious, I could feel underlying tension and fear. I sat down as she presented the coffee on a tray with cream and sugar bowls.

"Do you go out to a lot of haunted houses?" she began.

"Not as many in the winter, but I am called about once a week on a case." As I sipped my coffee I inquired, "How can I help you? Your phone call did not mention what it is all about. Fortunately I had nothing planned today but some paperwork that could be postponed."

"My husband thought I was crazy," she said. Her voice had changed; it seemed a scale higher. "But I saw it move." She pointed at the figure of a horse on one of the book cases and said, "I saw it float over to the floor by the fireplace." She told us other things had moved around. A tea pot in the kitchen was found on the floor in the corner. A bottle of perfume had moved from the bedroom to the hall. Some things had vanished.

She then said there were tappings, "As if someone was drumming their fingers on a hollow box." It would happen once or twice, then stop. She indicated that sometimes the walls seemed to shake. "Like an earthquake, then stop," she recalled. "Once it was violent enough to drop a picture from the wall."

I asked to see the picture that had fallen from the wall. She led me into the den with its leather furniture, walls of books and T.V. set. On the wall between two book cases was a print of a racing horse. "This one was found over there on the floor."

"The thing seems to dislike horses," I commented; thinking of the picture of the horse and the figurine in the living room. "Who else lives in the house?" I asked.

"Myself, my husband and our children, a son and a daughter." Both were in their teens.

"Is your son a silent type, but very creative? Does well in school but has few friends? Has he faced some stress lately?"

"No," she said. "He is outgoing and has many friends. He does like music and plays a guitar. He has even written some songs, but his grades are--well, he isn't an "A" student. Your description fits our daughter. She is the **real** student in the family."

"Has she had a difficult experience lately?" I asked.

"Yes, well a few weeks ago she broke up with her boyfriend."

I asked to see her room and was taken down a hall and into a cluttered room. Pictures of rock stars and posters filled the walls, a stereo system dominated one corner. Her bed was set against a wall that stood between her room and the den. Her pillow was near the place where the picture fell.

"You have a common poltergeist problem," I informed Mrs. B_____, "very common with adolescents about." I reassured her nothing evil would happen. "Poltergeists have been recorded for thousands of years and even though huge objects have been moved around, no one has been seriously injured. Most poltergeist phenomena last only three weeks or so."

"You mean this thing could just leave of its own accord?"

"Yes," I said, "and never come back."

The events occurred for about a week and then tapered off. In every incident the young lady in question was present.

We do not know the nature of the poltergeist, but observations have brought awareness of certain patterns--there is always a "focus," an individual where such things happen. And the events appear playful and mysterious.

After she was assured that she was not going mad and that the "haunting," if it could be called that, was temporary, I left. A call back confirmed my guess--the events slowly diminished and finally stopped in less than a week.

Once the spell of fear was lifted the home was on the way to recovery.

> The poltergeist is mischievous, destructive, noisy, cruel, thievish, malicious, audacious, ill-disposed, ruthless and vampiric: a ghost haunts, a poltergeist infests.
>
> --Harry Price

The Ghostly Children of Santa Barbara

The car head lamps pierced the night on the narrow road that wound back and forth in the hills above Santa Barbara. We were trying to locate a house plagued by a number of psychic phenomena described by the residents as "horrifying."

The two elderly residents had called me in the hope that I could dispel this haunting. I had gathered a crew of ghost hunters including a psychic and recording people.

We arrived at the home at 10:00 p.m. It was cold and crisp and breath steamed from our lips as we walked to the large home. After we knocked, the mahogany door opened to reveal two white haired ladies who peered nervously at us.

After introducing ourselves, we were ushered into the warm house. The ladies referred to themselves as Nell and Betty.

As in other visits, I asked if a tour could be made of the house before we spoke with them about their experiences. I did not want their comments to prejudice our group. Lead by a psychic, we began to tour the beautiful home. Antiques, works of art, and rich carpets dominated. The atmosphere reflected graciousness and good taste.

The bedroom we toured seemed different, strangely cold. My assistant seemed transfixed by the chair in the corner. As we walked into the room the icy coldness intensified. I checked the windows for drafts but was unable to find a cause.

The psychic stared into the room and when she reached the spot near the chair she announced, "It's holding my hand. It's a little boy. Oriental, maybe five years old." We continued our tour, but none of the other rooms turned up anything interesting.

Our party returned to the living room and we interviewed the two ladies.

"On the night of December 6, 1980, I was suddenly awakened from a sound sleep," began Betty. "I looked up and saw a woman standing in my bedroom. She was slender, wearing black bedroom slippers, a pink chiffon nightgown and ruffled bed cap. Her hair was grey and she seemed to be about 75 years of age. Her eyes were bright blue and she stared, but didn't blink. As I watched she groped her way along my closet door. I said, "Is that you, Nell?" Then she left, closing the door exactly as it had been."

This nocturnal visit was the beginning of a reign of terror.

Betty went on to describe how one of the figurines on the mantle suddenly moved. Nell explained how she looked up to see four young girls, Orientals, standing in the garden. As she tried to walk towards them they vanished into thin air. Nell also reported hearing and seeing a spectral young boy running down the hall waving a piece of paper. The ghostly child was also Oriental.

The fear in their eyes told us that these events were genuine and the cause of real concern to them. How much was real or imagined we could not know for certain, but one of our objectives was to relieve this fear and reassure them.

The psychic told them that she would try to release the spirit of the small boy she had felt in the bedroom. She told them that nothing in the house could harm them. The two women listened intently and seemed relieved. They were pleased that we did not judge them as others had.

After Mrs. P_____, the psychic, announced that the boy had left the house, we departed.

Was the house haunted? It seemed so to us; perhaps by memories of a Chinese community from long ago. Something was detected by the psychic who had no knowledge of the house, and the testimony of Nell and Betty of the Chinese specters confirmed her sighting.

> The spirit of the dead who stood in life before
> thee are again in death around thee, and their will
> shall overshadow thee; be still.
>
> Edgar Allan Poe

74

Ghost Lady of Santa Barbara City College

The view from this location was phenomenal. I could see the wharf, the marina, the palm-lined beach, the streets of Santa Barbara. On this bright and sunny day it seemed hard to believe that I was standing on a "haunted site." Many believe haunted places are always buildings or homes. This is far from the truth. Many are just places where activities once occurred that left a psychic scar. Such a place is Santa Barbara City College.

From the top of the bluff I could see why the Spanish built a small fort on the site two centuries ago. A horseshoe- shaped battery of bronze cannons defended Santa Barbara from foreigners, pirates or rebellious natives. From this position high on the bluff even a humble adobe bulwark could command the seaward approach to the city.

But my task today was not to study the history of Santa Barbara, but to examine the story of a ghost woman. I waited at the college for my informant to arrive. We had talked on the phone, but had not met in person. She had encountered an odd apparition. Jennifer T_____ was an art major at the college. It was while she was walking in the early evening that she chanced to see the phantom lady near the site of the old gun battery.

I waited for over an hour; always ready with a smile when a woman passed that I thought was my contact. But they returned my smile only and left. I was on the point of abandoning my vigil when a small woman bearing a huge portfolio came into view. She smiled and approached my bench. This must be Jennifer.

She introduced herself and explained that she had been late because of car trouble. We spoke about her classes and her previous experiences with the paranormal. A believer in astrology, she had had many psychic experiences including ESP with a sister and a boyfriend as well as an experience of premonition.

"I had this dream that I was listening to the radio once. . . in my room and they stopped the music and announced that John Lennon was shot. I woke up and told my friends and sister about it. It seemed so real. And two days later it happened--John Lennon was dead."

I asked if she had been listening to the radio when she received the report as she had in the dream.

"Yes," she assured me, "it was just like the dream."

When I asked her what she had experienced on the campus of the college, she pointed to a grassy area near the bluff. "I saw her right over there," she began.

"Why are you so sure it was a woman?" I asked, keeping up with her comments with my pen and pad.

"It was white, and flowing with long sleeves and a sort of shawl over the head. It seemed to walk about six inches above the ground as if it was as light as a feather."

"Did it look at you?" I inquired.

"I never saw her face. She walked over to the edge and looked out, then turned and vanished in a blue ball of light."

Being an art student, she made a pastel of the image she had seen. She withdrew it from her massive black portfolio case.

"This is what I saw." It featured a night sky and the whitish form with one alabaster arm out and the long gown-like garment streaming in the wind; a haunting illustration. I asked if she would part with the picture.

"No," she explained with a smile, "it's my first ghost."

Others have reported ghosts at the site. Some say it is the restless spirit of an Indian woman who was killed by the Spanish here almost 200 years ago. Others contend that the woman is the ghost of one of the soldier's wives who died during childbirth and is seeking her husband who was stationed at the installation. Jennifer's description seemed to confirm the latter tale. The dress was more like that of a Spanish woman than an Indian maiden.

> You may talk to the dead but the dead
> do not answer.
>> Harry Houdini

Crying Child of Mission Santa Barbara

The beautiful twin towers of Mission Santa Barbara have fascinated visitors for almost two centuries. The Mission stands as a symbol of the entire chain built by the Spanish padres in California. I drove into the parking lot of the busy Mission, finding a vacant spot near the old stone fountain.

Tourists filled the place on this warm summer day, but I was not here to enjoy the peaceful atmosphere of the historic Mission. I was here to study the report of a psychic phenomena experienced on the grounds.

"I have something on tape I want you to hear!" Donald K_____ said excitedly over the phone that morning. "I have the crying of a phantom baby." Donald was a student of the paranormal and was studying reports of hauntings in the Santa Barbara and San Luis Obispo areas. An amateur, he made up for his lack of training and experience with enthusiasm and hard work. I saw Donald standing by the door of the gift shop of the old Mission. His bony frame reminded me of a sketch of young Abraham Lincoln.

"I have it right here," he announced, patting his portable tape recorder. I captured the crying sounds in the graveyard of the Mission."

We entered the Mission, passing through the displays in the building's colorful museum. The museum chronicled the history of the establishment from its founding on December 4th, 1786 to its restoration. We did not pause to examine the many artifacts and photographs. Our goal was the old walled cemetery beside the Mission church. The cemetery is a peaceful place where many of California's pioneer families lie beside the mortal remains of some 4,000 local Indians who labored and perished at this Mission. Many stories of ghosts are associated with the missions of California. Perhaps these tales were inspired by the cemeteries built beside the old churches. The venerable churches were among the oldest structures in the state. Santa Barbara has several tales of wandering phantoms. Several are rumored to haunt the Mission's graveyard.

Donald took me to an aged tombstone in the back of the enclosed cemetery. "It was here," he indicated, "I set up the tape recorder and got the sounds of a crying baby. It sounds like a very young child." With that he pressed the "play" button and an odd cry issued from the speaker. It did resemble the sob of an infant. It was eerie! He played it a second time. I suddenly laughed. My childhood in Thousand Oaks, California had taken me many times to the wild animal compound called "Jungleland" where my father worked for a while. I had heard the sound on the tape many often at "Jungleland."

"It's a peacock," I blurted out. "It's the cry of a peacock."

"Peacock," he said with a curious look, "No, no, it's a baby crying; you're wrong."

"No," I smiled. I know a peacock when I hear one. I'm sorry, but I don't think you have a ghost there unless it's the ghost of a peacock."

"Peacocks only live in Africa," he answered.

"India," I corrected.

"Well in any case they are not native to California," he added in defense of his tape. "Where could it have come from? There are no peacocks here--you're wrong."

As if on cue, a majestic blue peacock strutted out from behind some flowers and looked at us with his cocked head. I had to control my friend as he started to toss the tape recorder at the bird.

The Ghosts of Las Cruces

The wind tugged at my hair as I walked towards what was left of a community called Las Cruces, a town that died a true "ghost town."

Located at the entrance of the windy Gaviota pass, the tiny hamlet can be located only on older maps of Santa Barbara County. Las Cruces was displaced by the 101 Freeway. The name of the town is derived from a tragedy which may explain the ghostly happenings reported today. Legend states that when gray robed Franciscans explored this area, they found many graves marked with wooden crosses. It was believed that Spanish soldiers had fought a battle with the local Indians and that the soldiers, armed with muskets, had overcome the natives. The Spanish buried the fallen Indians, giving each a Christian burial. The Spanish built an adobe building here. It was later replaced by a larger adobe that served as a stage coach stop, saloon, and hotel. As time passed the old adobe became a gambling hall with a reputation of being one of the wildest whiskey emporiums on the coast. The adobe was widely known as a place of loose women and strong brew. Eventually it became a brothel.

The ghosts reported by a group of local psychics indicates that they originated in the last period of the adobe's operation. The two spirits seen around the crumbling walls were two women who once worked there and were strangled by a deranged man. Another report claims that the ghost is that of a girl who grew despondent about her sad life and hanged herself in the adobe. One lady who visited the site said that she saw a tall man standing amid the ruins in a black frock coat; perhaps the victim of a gambling shootout. Upon hearing such stories and legends I knew I would visit the site.

I sat among the broken boards and crumbling ruins trying to imagine the tragedies and events that happened within the walls. It was easy to imagine the ghosts of long dead cowboys and dance hall girls mingling with the whistling winds that came down Gaviota Pass.

I closed my eyes and sat quietly trying to experience the ghosts of this ruined place. I began to feel I was being watched. Then a sudden chill thrilled me. Could it be that the legends and stories were true? Could it be that the restless spirits of Las Cruces had heard my prayers and were now about to reveal themselves to me?

I opened my eyes and saw a movement on the grass, a shadow, then a piercing feminine scream filled the air. I leaped up. High above a sea gull cried again. Were the ghostly shadows and sounds only the birds soaring in the winds? I wasn't certain.

> He who does not fill his world
> with phantoms remains alone.
> --Antonio Porchia

The Haunted Hacienda

The adobe did not look over 150 years old, but the rain that thundered around us as we turned up the dirt road made any architectural examination difficult. As lightning and thunder cracked around the hilltop ranch near Lompoc, we made a wet run through the rain and mud to the long porch. We had reached our objective; the old Spanish adobe that was the center of the alleged haunting.

My crew of psychics and photographers were ready. This case offered us a challenge. Not only did the thick walls contain a phantom, but the owners claimed a terrible curse had struck down those who examined too closely the history of the site. Beside the curse, rumor held that a golden treasure was buried somewhere on the property--a treasure believed to be worth $5,000 in gold!   We were met by the owner and his wife and ushered into the well-furnished historic building. We were offered coffee and tea and seated in the living room. The owner then began to tell of his experiences at the ranch.

I felt as if I had been thrust into a grade "B" horror film. I sat on an overstuffed chair in a lavish 150 year old adobe as rain pelted the windowpanes and a fire crackled in the hearth. Before me sat a young, upper middle class and well educated family, telling me of a dreadful curse, a lost treasure, and a haunting phantom.   Their story was interrupted frequently by thunder and lightning.

"Don Pablo cursed this land." Mr. M_____ continued, "From that day on no Anglo to own the place has prospered. Don Pablo was an emissary for the King of Spain. For his services, he was granted this Rancho of 16,000 acres. He built this adobe near the site of an Indian village. He raised sheep and cattle and was content until bad times came forcing Don Pablo to borrow money from an American. When Don Pablo sold his cattle that next spring he offered to repay the loan of $5,000, but the American insisted that he pay an additional $500 for interest. In Spanish California a borrower was not charged interest, but in American California that changed. The American insisted that he receive the interest on the next day or he would foreclose on the entire Rancho.

"Don Pablo grew incensed and took the $5,000 in gold and buried it on the grounds. He told his trusted Indian servant his curse that, 'No Anglo will own this land!' He went out to a large

81

tree and hanged himself! Any Anglo who has owned the ranch has come to grief. Slowly parts of the ranch have been sold off. The adobe hacienda and lands were once owned by a Cooper family who used the property as a sheep ranch until the family's oldest son died of diphtheria. When he became ill, the father sent his ranch foreman to Santa Barbara for the doctor. He had traveled that road many times but that night he became lost and failed to bring the doctor in time to save the boys life. The Coopers, in their grief, abandoned the ranch. Success did not come to the ranch until it was purchased by the Silva family. Not being Anglos they were exempt from the curse. That is, until Mr. Silva became interested in the legend and started to search for the treasure. Then he became strangely ill, a sickness that was cured only when he moved from the adobe. Others had suffered losses here, accidents, and bad luck. We did not believe in curses and all that. . . but lately things have been happening!"

The ranch hands had been talking of the curse and the wandering specter of Don Pablo. A high percentage of accidents were reported and several horses were strangely injured. These events as well as the fears of the ranch hands were enough for them to contact me.

When I asked if my group could tour the old adobe, we were escorted through the large U shaped building. The psychic, Mrs. P_____, saw a figure with a baggy shirt and an odd hat. She sensed his pride. The others confirmed a strange chill in several rooms of the house. The wife of Mr. M_____ told of hearing noises--the sounds of people talking--and informed us that the ranch workers had seen a whitish form they referred to as Don Pablo.

Something was present, of that we were sure. But what was it and why did it haunt this site? Was there really a curse? We left the adobe after making arrangements to return in a week. We wanted time to study the records and learn of Don Pablo, emissary from Spain.

Research in the archives in Santa Barbara did record such an individual, but they stated that he did not commit suicide:

> Jan. 5, 1801 The commander of the presidio
> (Santa Barbara) informed the governor that
> Ensign Pablo, three soldiers and a colonist
> had died of catarrh and pleurisy.

The early period was decades before the American occupation of California (1847) and seemed to rule out the legend of the borrowed gold. The story of the curse did not agree with the recorded history of the site. We returned and reviewed the data we had found. It was at this point that psychic, Mrs. P_____, made an interesting discovery. The image she had observed had been wearing an odd hat, a derby. Few Spanish ranchero's wore that type of head gear. Looking through some of the photos of the ranch we discovered a picture of Mr. Cooper, the man who tried sheep ranching on the site in the late 19th century. The picture showed him wearing a derby!

Based upon the evidence of the hat, it was suggested that the phantom was Mr. Cooper, who was attached by grief to the place where his son had died tragically. We prescribed that the family have the house blessed by a Catholic priest--the faith of the family--and that a short service be held to release the sad spirit. After these measures were taken, the ranch was lifted from its pall of fear. The ranch hands reported no ghostly figure and good fortune blessed the owners. The curse, or fear of it, was lifted.

> My people too were scared with eerie sounds,
> A foot step, a low throbbing in the walls,
> A noise of falling weights that never fell,
> Weird whispers, bell that rang without a hand,
> Door-handles turn'd when none was at the door,
> And bolted doors that open'd of themselves;
> And on betwixt the dark and light had seen
> Her, bending by the cradle of her babe.
> > --Tennyson,
> > **The Ring**

The Ghosts of La Purisima

Something was amiss, but perhaps it was only a stray breeze of crisp January air that sent a sudden chilling sensation down my spine. I stood alone looking at the restored buildings that make up the complex of Mission La Purisima Concepcion, located in Santa Barbara County near Lompoc. They appeared stark and foreboding on this cold and damp morning.

The rest of my team of students and psychic researchers was late in beginning the investigation of this historic site. As the wind chilled me again, I decided to walk into the nearest adobe structure for protection against the numbing cold. I had heard stories of the ghosts of La Purisima for many years. There were always wild tales that seemed hardly creditable; stories of headless monks and moaning Indian spirits. But as the wind howled the stories seemed more and more believable. Others who investigated the historic mission came away convinced that ghosts do wander the grounds; others are equally convinced that the reports are greatly exaggerated. If the Mission did indeed hold a phantom congregation, my team was determined to confirm or deny its existence.

As I wandered through the restored rooms of what had been workshops, I recalled the history of the place. Founded in 1787, La Purisima was the eleventh mission built in California. It was destroyed in the terrible earthquake of 1812 and rebuilt on the present site, a short distance away. The mission prospered for a decade until drought, fires, frosts, floods, epidemics, and Indian revolt devastated it. Fray Mariano Payeras labored hard to make the Mission a success until he died there on April 28, 1823. He lies buried beneath the altar of the church he built. After his death, slow decay settled over the complex until it was sold by the Mexican government in 1834. Abandoned, it stood for over half a century as a crumbling adobe ruin with only ghosts and an occasional traveler to walk its dark halls.

The buildings were almost gone when restoration began in the late 1930s. La Purisima State Historic Park is now fully restored and open to the public as a museum. While walking through the rooms, I felt watched by unseen eyes. The realistic reconstruction gave me the eerie sensation that the inhabitants had simply walked away leaving their tools and possessions behind. The dark rooms were cold and offered scant protection from the icy winds. I walked to the end of the corridor and out the open doorway. Before me loomed the mission church. Suddenly, the wind swept open my jacket in a strong blast. I had the uncanny feeling that something was watching from the church building.

Glancing back towards the parking lot I saw two members of my team arrive. Turning from the church I retraced my steps across the wind-swept grounds to the parking lot where others began to arrive. Soon we could commence our investigation.

The group of twenty-two included psychics, artists, photographers and students from my class on the paranormal. They carried the equipment needed to conduct a psychic investigation: cameras, pens and pads of paper, portable tape recorders and thermometers. I deliberately kept the group ignorant of the site and its background lest I prejudice them or give fuel to overly active imaginations. Each of the group was given forms to fill out that included a map of the mission complex. They were instructed to mark any place they felt might be haunted and to record all feelings and impressions. The team was divided into pairs; each pair operating independently. I requested that each pair keep all findings from the other groups until the forms were completed. The pairs were given an hour to tour the Mission and make their reports. We would meet in the walled cemetery and discuss our findings, if any.

I anticipated patterns to develop. Eleven groups, all with little or no background, should select random sites. But if a majority identified one location, it might indicate a psychic disturbance. At the least it would be a good starting place for our investigation.

I walked into the gardens and found a seat on a bench amid the wind blown plants. The sun was attempting to come out from the clouds, but even this could not dispel the odd feeling that engulfed me. The groups were now on their own. From my vantage point I could see the members of my team moving about the Mission buildings, clipboards at the ready, cameras clicking and flashing. I did not want my presence to influence them in any way.

As I waited in the cold dusty garden, I could not shake the image of the Mission church. The long building seemed to beckon me. No matter how I turned, I found myself staring at that one structure. The wind blew again, sending grainy dust into my eyes.

At last I made my way to the walled graveyard where hundreds of mission Indians found their last resting place. Slowly, in groups of twos, my team sought shelter from the wind behind a thick wall. They handed in their maps and forms. Each map was decorated with crosses where they felt a psychic disturbance. As I glanced over the sheets, I was surprised to notice a pattern developing. A large percentage had selected the Mission church as a haunted location. When the others arrived we discussed what they had experienced.

Mrs. O_____, a psychic with the gift of clairvoyance, reported a strange sensation as she entered the church. "It was a sadness. . . a sudden sadness. As I walked into the church I was surprised to smell sweet flowers and looking around I could sense colors--bright colors on the walls, lots of reds and blues. The walls were once brightly painted. . . not like they are today. As I approached the altar rail of the church, I felt the sadness returning. I looked back and the walls were splashed with color, then it was just gone." Mrs. O_____ was raised on the East Coast of the United States and had no knowledge of the missions of California or the color found in Catholic churches of the Southwest.

Another couple, Mr. and Mrs. R_____ had another experience in the church. "There is something there. I felt it," began the husband, an engineer by profession. "I definitely felt a cold spot near a nitch in the wall as well as in the front of the church. It was creepy in there." His wife confirmed his feelings. She felt something in the rear of the building. "It made my skin crawl," she added.

Another team reported a remarkable sighting. Mr. S_____ experienced an image or vision inside the church. He left his team mate and wandered alone into the deserted church. He turned and was shocked to see the apparitions of "many small Indians crouching or kneeling on the floor. "The Indians did not look at me. They were dressed in rags and had long dirty hair. The rags were a dirty grey and some of them were wrapped with torn brown blankets. The Indians had flat faces. One was covered with marks. . . marks on his face like pimples. One wore a wide yellow headband. Their hair was almost a foot long and matted: they looked wretched." This description did not match the colorful dioramas and displays of well-dressed, happy mission Indians shown at the small museum on the grounds. Mr. S_____ was convinced that the vision he had seen for a few seconds in the church was a true image from the past.

Another psychic, Mrs. P_____, had toured the church and reported odd feelings in the building. She felt a number of cold spots, and the image of a statue that should have stood in an empty nitch. She felt an oppressive feeling of guilt in the rear of the church.

More than two-thirds of the group had experienced something in the church from mild apprehension to sudden panic and fear. It was decided that, although other locations had been selected as well, the majority favored the adobe church as a potential "haunted site." We gathered our gear and returned in silence to the chapel.   Perhaps it was only suggestion, but I felt an odd tingling as I crossed the threshold into the barn-like structure. It was cold in the damp chamber--the cold of a tomb. Little light filtered in through the high narrow windows. The air was strong with the musty odor of wet mold and damp adobe. The eye was pulled to the altar where statues gazed back in unblinking silence. No pews broke the emptiness of the floor. Only a tiled floor served the Indians of yesteryear. Going into the dim church was like being swallowed by an immense living creature.

The team slowly spread out trying to locate the cold spots detected by the psychics in our group. It was not long before someone felt an invisible cylinder of icy cold. We gathered around the spot. We could feel the coldness as we passed our hands through the phenomena. Using thermometers we attempted to measure the temperature of the thing with little luck. Only a slight variance was recorded. Several other cold spots were felt until five were detected and their locations charted on graph paper.

One of the psychics seemed frozen before the altar, staring with wide-eyed fascination at the tomb of Fray Mariano Payeras. "Something is wrong," she murmured. "Something is wrong with this grave. I can't put my finger on it but, something is wrong. He doesn't belong here."

We left the chapel and found one of the volunteer docents who give tours of the historic mission. We asked if he had heard stories of ghosts here at La Purisima. We were seeking independent confirmation of the events recorded in the church. The docent was amused at our question. "We get a lot of questions about our ghosts," he said with a smile. I turned on my portable tape recorder to tape his answer. "Mostly around Halloween. We get a lot of local newspaper people taking pictures. I have never seen a ghost here myself and I have been over here late at night, but I have talked with a few who swear that there are ghosts here. There is one story that a ghostly gardener is seen from time to time working on the grounds with his hoe. Some say that the ghost of old Don Vincente haunts the kitchen building where he was murdered back around a hundred and fifty years ago."

"There is also a legend about a ghostly bandit on horseback seen riding back and forth before the mission buildings late at night. They say he is guarding a treasure he buried under one of the brick pillars. I have never talked with anyone who has seen him."

I asked if there were any stories of ghosts seen in the church building. He only smiled, "I haven't heard of any," he replied with a grin. We thanked him for his time and gathered in the mission gardens to conclude our "ghost hunt." The on-site investigation was done, but the difficult part of the research and confirmation was beginning. As we left the Mission I could not resist a last look at the foreboding church.

One of the least talked about parts of psychic investigation is research. It can be time consuming, frustrating, and at times painfully boring. But it is important to study the background of a location and discover if the events witnessed have some basis in fact.

The missions of California have been the topics of research for over a hundred years, so it did not prove difficult to uncover a few known facts.

Going through old newspapers and local accounts, I soon learned that the phantom outlaw said to ride at the mission had been an elaborate hoax developed by a local newspaper man decades ago. The story of the murdered Don Vincente was more promising. It was based upon oral accounts from the last century and may have reflected a real event.

In analyzing the past of the church, I was rewarded by findings; a few facts that confirmed some of the reported impressions. It was likely that the walls had been colorfully painted in the past. Two of the most prominent colors were red and blue. The historic record also indicates that the mission suffered tremendous hardships and the Indian population faced extreme poverty. Many times clothing and blankets were in short supply. Disease was common to the mission Indians; many were taken by smallpox. This would confirm the wretched apparitions seen by the psychic. The marks on the face could have been pockmarks from smallpox. Hundreds of ill-clothed, undernourished Indians lived their short lives in the shadow of the Mission church. Perhaps within its thick walls they enjoyed a moment of peace in a life of hardship.

During the weeks of research I met a man, Mr. D_____, who lives in Ventura. He had worked on the restoration of La Purisima while a member of the C.C.C. back in 1940. He told me that several odd things occurred during the reconstruction.

"While we were working on the church we took up the old Spanish tile floor. Underneath some of the tiles we found small skeletons of infants or small children. It was thought that they had been buried there by the Indians after the church had been abandoned. The local Indians still thought of the church as a holy place--what better location to bury a precious child taken so young by God."

I asked Mr. D_____ if he could recall how many were found. He said about four or five. I quickly produced the map we had made of the cold spots. To the best of his recollection, our map marked the sites of the infant burials!

Research on Fray Payeras was also interesting. Records indicate that he has two graves! One in La Purisima and another at Mission Santa Barbara. When the body of the good padre was exhumed, it proved rather mysterious. The upper half of the priest was discovered in the church at La Purisima, but from the waist down the skeleton was missing. It was later discovered at Mission Santa Barbara. Why was the missionary cut in half? Why the two graves? Perhaps this is why there is no peace in the Mission church, why something is disturbing the site. The psychic had been correct that the grave was amiss.

One of the goals of the investigation was to prove or disprove the stories of ghosts at the restored mission. Based upon the evidence collected and researched, I must conclude that La Purisima Concepcion is indeed a much haunted site. The tragedies that mar the history of this Mission have left a psychic scar that may not heal for eons.

> The most beautiful thing we can experience
> is the mysterious. It is the source of all true
> art and science.
> > --Albert Einstein
> > "What I Believe," **Forum**

The Black Coach of Santa Ynez

Y ou're going to think we're crazy, but we really saw it." Her
eyes flashed as we sipped our drinks in the rustic atmosphere of
Mattie's Tavern in the small town of Los Olivos, north of Santa
Barbara.

"Terri and I were within twenty feet of the thing when it
passed by," Bob H_____ said. He held his young wife's hand as
he described the incident that lead them to call me. "The
strangest thing about it was the silence--it was absolutely silent."
"We were just outside Santa Ynez going towards Solvang. . .
when we had a flat on the Volvo. It must have been about 8:00
or 8:30 in the evening. There was still some light and I was
changing the tire. I had the car on the jack when Terri called
my attention to it."

"It was like a black cloud coming towards us," she
interrupted, "It was moving fast."

"I came over to her side of the car," he continued, "in time
to see this big black thing coming parallel to the road. It looked
like an old coach pulled by four horses... all black. There was a
guy on top, a driver I guess, he was wearing a sort of top hat,
you know, like Lincoln wore, and a long black coat."

"It wasn't a stagecoach," Terri insisted, "no, I've seen
stagecoaches before in Knott's Berry Farm. This was, square and
black."

"Did it have large windows on the sides?" I asked, thinking
what they were describing resembled a nineteenth century hearse.

"It was more like a carriage," answered Bob.

"Could it have been a hearse? An old horse drawn hearse?"
I inquired.

"No," Bob replied, "no, it was a carriage." His wife nodded
in agreement.

"What else can you tell me about this apparition?"

"Well," Bob started, as he sketched a drawing on a piece of
napkin, "it had lights on the side and doors with windows."

"Was there anyone inside?" I asked.

"Yes," blurted Terri, "a woman in a black dress--an old
woman, maybe ninety. I just saw her for a second as it went by."

"I didn't see anyone inside; I guess I wasn't looking for
that," confessed Bob. "It went by just too fast."

Bob finished his sketch of the dark carriage. It was very
square with large wheels in the back; totally enclosed. It did not

resemble any stagecoaches I had seen.

"The coach went past us, dead silent; not a sound and then headed off towards Santa Inez. It slowly vanished into the dusk."

"What did you do then?" I asked.

"What do you think?" he stammered. "I changed the tire and got back on the highway. We didn't stop until we were back home."

Bob and Terri are both college graduates with professional careers. Bob had not experienced this type of event and was mystified by the encounter. They called friends who recommended they contact me. We agreed on a meeting near the site of this odd manifestation.

"Black coaches have been seen for centuries," I explained. "They are far more common in Ireland and Great Britain than here in the United States. One interesting feature is that it made absolutely no sound. This is common with other sightings of phantom coaches.

Legends hold that such ghostly vehicles carry away the souls of the dead and that they are seen when someone has passed away. Yet, there could be another explanation. It is believed by some parapsychologists that occasionally images from the past can intrude into the present. Sort of like a bit of film accidentally replaying at the wrong time. This glimpse of the past is called 'retrocognition'."

"You think this might be that?" Terri asked sipping her gin and tonic.

"It's possible," I assured her. "Still, the local Indians tell of a black coach too. This all-black carriage is always driven by a man in a tall black hat." Bob's eyes opened wide as he finished his drink. "The ghost coach is said to be driven by the Devil himself, who takes the souls of evil people back with him to hell."

After finishing our drinks we drove their car through Los Olivos to the lonely road outside Santa Ynez. We pulled off into the wide space where the couple remembered encountering the black coach. I got out of the car and walked across the road. The sun was setting in a splash of orange and pink, the cool of dusk was replacing the summer heat. I could see for miles in either direction. I stood staring into the setting sun hoping the dark carriage would appear. A truck, several cars and a camper towing a boat roared past, but no phantom coach appeared. But then, perhaps no evil persons had died today and the Devil could take the day off from his hellish taxi service. It was dark when we left the site. We continued to Solvang and enjoyed a fine dinner where I tried to get across my non-judgmentalness in regard to their unshakable conviction as to what they had seen.

> Tis strange, but true; for truth is always
> strange--
> Stranger than fiction.
>
> > --Lord Byron,
> > **Don Juan**

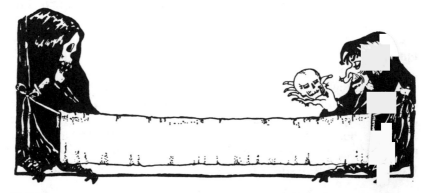

The Haunted Tavern of Guadalupe

It's haunted all right and I wouldn't go back to work there for a million dollars." His eyes were cold and steady. He had volunteered his story over coffee one rainy afternoon in the small community of Guadalupe in northern Santa Barbara County. "I tell you it is haunted because I heard him," continued the young man.

My goal in coming to the town had not been to find a haunted tavern. I was seeking information on "the Lost City of the Pharaohs," located in the nearby sand dunes. The 'Hollywood' city was originally constructed for a Cecil B. DeMill classic silent film, **The Ten Commandments** (not to be confused with the remake he directed years later with a young Charleton Heston). Storms later buried it under the sand. I was having no luck finding the movie set of the Egyptian city, but I was fortunate in meeting several people who told of the ghost at the Far West Tavern. I had heard several accounts when I met Mr. R_____ who had worked there. When he proved to be talkative, we had coffee and donuts and I interviewed him.

"You see, it was not always a restaurant. Originally, long ago, it was a hotel. That's when 'Mr. Franconeti' lived there. He was a nice old man. He had lost his leg in World War I and had a peg leg. Well, he died in the hotel when it caught fire in the 1930s and his ghost walks the upper rooms. You can hear him walkin' around. Thump-bump, thump-bump. He couldn't get out in time, so he was burned to death. That's why he is haunting the place. Later it was rebuilt as a restaurant. There is a cold spot in the upstairs room--that marks where he died. Everyone who works over there has heard or seen Mr. Franconeti. One guy heard him coming down for him and left. Even the manager has seen it. Objects would move around. Once the big steer head they have nailed to the wall was found turned upside down! I saw something dark move in the back room--I thought it was one of the guys who work there, but it wasn't them. It was nothing. So I quit."

I went over to the restaurant, a fine steak house where drinks and well-cooked slabs of beef are offered at a modest price. I saw the steer head and patrolled the premises. I found one upstairs room slightly colder than the rest, but I failed to hear the distinct walk of Mr. Franconeti. Still, the place had a certain atmosphere about it. Perhaps--late at night--when the

93

lights are down low? Who knows? Maybe Mr. Franconeti's ghost does indeed walk.

I'm inclined to think we are all ghosts--
every one of us.

--Henrik Ibsen

Ghosts and Hauntings
of
San Luis Obispo County

I have often, while sitting in the parlor, in the day time, had a perception that somebody was passing the windows--but, on looking toward them, nobody is there.

--Nathaniel Hawthorne

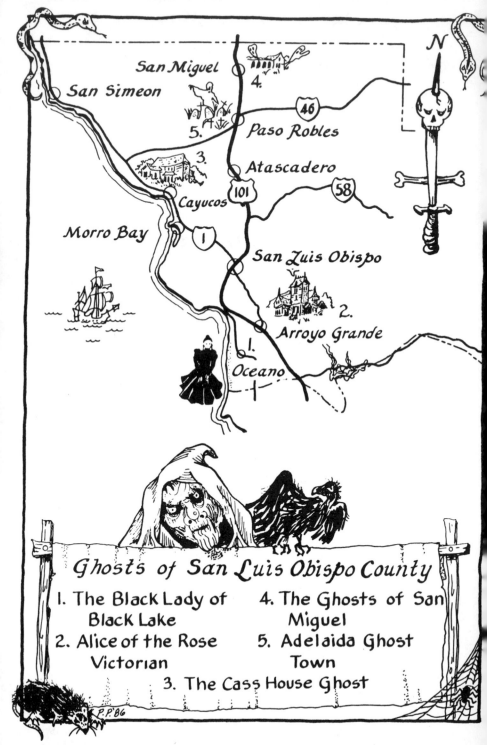

N

San Miguel
San Simeon
4.
46
5.
Paso Robles
3.
Atascadero
101
Cayucos
58
Morro Bay
1
San Luis Obispo
2.
Arroyo Grande
1.
Oceano

Ghosts of San Luis Obispo County

1. The Black Lady of Black Lake
2. Alice of the Rose Victorian
3. The Cass House Ghost
4. The Ghosts of San Miguel
5. Adelaida Ghost Town

P.P. '86

The Black Lake Lady

Driving slowly along Highway One, we were constantly aware of the time. The ghost lady is rumored to appear precisely at 12:30 at night. The three of us, packed into my small car, had our cameras ready for any chance sighting of the mysterious ghost. The dark lady is said to walk on the still surface of Black Lake, one of the seven dune lakes, that lies in the Oceano sand dunes south of Pismo Beach. Legend states that the Black Lake is bottomless. Most experts agree that it is shallow, but who can say for certain?

The black-garbed lady is rumored to have drowned in this body of water almost two hundred years ago. This night Mrs. G_____ and Miss T_____ had joined in the investigation of the phenomenon. The dark specter had been brought to my attention by one of my former students who had seen the apparition two years before.

A former resident of Pismo Beach, Miss T_____ had heard of a number of local encounters with the lady some refer to as 'Agnes'.

"Four of us saw her. She was standing out by the reeds just standing on the water. At first I thought it was only a shadow or a clump of brush, but then she started to move. She seemed to float a few inches over the water towards us." Miss T_____ began to tell of the frightful night when she and three friends saw the Black Lake phantom.

"How was it dressed?" I asked taking notes and recording her account.

"She was all in black with a long full skirt. I could not see her feet. She had a very small waist. The dress went up to her neck and had long tight sleeves with black lace on the cuffs."

The girl kept looking out the window toward the haunted lake, as if she were describing the apparition by sight and not from memory.

"Her hair was done up high on her head in a sort of bun and she wore long black earrings that shined with black jewels. And, and, she had no face. Nothing, just a white light where a face should be."

I had heard of faceless phantoms before; many seem linked to the Hispanic culture. Ghosts of this type are found throughout the Southwest and Latin America. Why faceless? Miss T_____'s account fits well into the Hispanic pattern. She was of Mexican

97

heritage. The woman was convinced she had seen a ghost. We got out of the car and walked under the light of the full moon towards the lake.

"It's almost 12:30," I said. "Do you know why she comes out at that time?"

"That's when she was murdered," answered Miss T_____. "They say that if you drive Highway One along here at 12:30 she will appear in the roadway too. There are many accidents along this highway."

Mrs. G_____, a sensitive, was meditating, staring into the dark waters of the mysterious lake. "Do you feel something?" I inquired. She did not answer. We waited as I tensely watched my timepiece, waiting for the fateful 12:30. "I want to go," protested Miss T_____. "I don't want to see her again. Let's go."

"Just a moment," I said, "Just a minute more and it will be 12:30. That's why we came out here, remember? Don't worry, the dead cannot harm the living."

"Are you sure?" she asked with a tremble. I hoped that I was.

Slowly the second hand made its sweep across the face of my watch. Finally it reached 12:30. Cameras ready, we looked in every direction.

"O God! O God!" Miss T_____ started to sob. Perhaps it was her cries that alarmed the ducks in the marshlands. We will never know for certain, but as she cried out a number of them bolted from the reeds and grasses. My heart leaped up into my throat as I heard the crashing reeds and water. My feet seemed set in cement as I glanced right and left expecting the black lady to be swooping down upon me.

Miss T_____ screamed and ran to the car with Mrs. G_____ close behind. I was left alone--alone with the ducks and perhaps the terrible phantom. I saw nothing, but the hair on the back of my neck started to rise. The air took on a definite chill as my hearing seemed to become acute. I jumped when I heard the car motor crank up. I headed back not wishing to be stranded by the shores of haunted Black Lake. I saw nothing. But as I returned to the car, I felt watched and had to suppress a desire to run. Perhaps the spirit of drowned Agnes was watching from the reeds.

Black Lake Lady

Alice, the Ghost of the Rose Victorian Inn

We lost our direction three times in trying to locate our destination in the community of Arroyo Grande in San Luis Obispo County. We were beginning to believe that the existence of the haunted mansion, like a phantom, was open to speculation when we rounded a corner and observed the lofty pink spire that dominated the countryside. It was unmistakable. The three storied, turreted pile of the Rose Victorian Inn loomed up, unashamedly ornate.

That day I had brought with me a gifted psychic, Debbie Christenson. As she had taken my class and proved invaluable on a number of ghost hunts, it was decided she should accompany me on a full fledged ghost investigation. With no prior knowledge of the site, this would be a test of her psychic abilities.

The present owners of the Rose Victorian Inn have operated it for several years as a bed and breakfast establishment. In the years of operation, they learned from their guests that a ghost seemed to inhabit the tower room. They invited me to investigate the sightings and determine if there was indeed a ghost.

Debbie gazed, transfixed, as we pulled up to the huge mansion, which was painted in several shades of pink. "There is something in that house," she said rubbing her hands together.

I had done some research on the gabled house. Built in 1885 as the main house of a large walnut farm, it was restored in the late 1950s. Part of it was used as a steak house in the 1960s. The restaurant addition is now used for those who stay at the Inn. Debbie and I introduced ourselves and asked if we could tour the mansion and discover what Debbie could sense using her psychic gifts. Going through the house was like walking back in time to another era. Samplers, plush chairs, antiques made one think of a slower time when grace and hospitality were commonplace. I had warned the owners to say nothing about the ghost as we toured the building lest it influence Debbie. After the tour we could discuss our findings.

The psychic stared at the staircase and began to tremble. "It's, it's a little girl," she said in amazement. "I can see her. She is standing on the staircase."   I   looked   and   saw nothing. "Where," I asked, "Where is she?" Debbie pointed to the newelpost. I walked towards it.

"She is laughing," Debbie remarked, "she knows you can't see her. Now she's running up the stairs." Debbie's eyes followed an invisible image as it went halfway up the staircase.

I asked Debbie to ask the girl her name.

"Alice," she replied. "She looks about nine years old. She is wearing pigtails, long dress, small apron."

Next Debbie dashed up the stairs, I in close pursuit with my notebook. She turned a corner then up a narrow flight that ended in the narrow confines of the tower room.

Debbie stopped at the door. "This is her room," she said. "She is there by the window; she likes to look out." I could still see nothing, but a sudden chill did strike me--was it my imagination?

"She likes cats," stated the psychic. "She loves to pet them. She doesn't know she is dead and she is waiting."

I asked what she was waiting for.

"She is waiting for her mother, but she likes the other one; the lady who cleans and takes care of the house. The lady has short hair and is a bit chunky. The lady can't see her, but Alice follows her around... She also likes the little boy, but he is too shy to come out now. But they play on the roof."

The ghostly child seemed an innocent prankster from Debbie's description. But I had only the psychic's word for what she had seen. We went downstairs to talk with the owners. Their description of the girl Alice matched the reports they received of the sightings in the house. The owners were amazed by the reference to cats. They had discovered that cats had a strange love of the tower room and were often in there sleeping near the window.

They were also surprised by the description of the woman loved by the mysterious little girl: it matched that of the housekeeper who was away for the day. "Wait a moment," said the owner's wife. She soon returned with a large blow-up of an old photograph. The picture showed the mansion as it looked many decades ago. But in the photograph, at one of the upper windows a small grey form looked down. It was the form of what appeared to be a little girl with pig tails!

The Rose Victorian Inn on Valley Road, Arroyo Grande is indeed a haunted house--haunted by the memories of another time and yes, perhaps by the laughing echoes of a young girl who will never grow old.

Ghosts only come to those who look for them.
Old German saying

Captain Cass's House

I t's for sale, you know," the lady said with the sort of smile made by people who smile too much to make a sale. "Nice and roomy and oh, the history." She waved her hands and walked with us to the remnants of what had once been a fence of some kind. "It would take a lot of work, but just think of the memories these walls hold." Debbie the psychic, now a good friend from Camarillo, smiled at me and whispered, "Think of the nightmares it holds."

The Cass house looked like the traditional haunted house of film and fiction. Peeling paint and broken windows gave it a certain decadent look, yet a feeling that it was indeed not empty--not empty at all.

We had met Mrs. N_____ at the local pier near to the community of Cayucos in San Luis Obispo County. She had been asking some of the local businessmen about the old Cass house, having heard stories in Morro Bay of its odd ghost. Mrs. N_____ had overheard our inquiries and taken it upon herself to show us around. She was a professional woman who found time to vacation in the Cayucos area and was well versed in its history.

"The Cass house is beautiful," she said, "someone should do something to save the old thing." She lead us up Ocean Avenue to the two-storied home.

"Built in 1867, it was made of wood imported from San Francisco by steamship. It was the finest home in the area for many years," she continued gesturing to the peeling wooden porch. She seemed to enjoy her role as a lecturer and it betrayed the actress that lurked within her soul.

"The house was built by Capt. James Cass who founded the town of Cayucos and some say that late at night he walks the halls of the house. As the captain walks he is always looking out to sea as if he is waiting for a storm or for a ship to come in."

As Debbie went forward and peered into one of the dirty cracked windows, I asked, "Have you seen the Captain?"

"No, I don't believe in that nonsense, but people have reported some odd things inside this old house and, well, if there is a ghost inside these walls it wouldn't surprise me one bit."

Mrs. N_____ walked me around the back of the mansion to where Debbie was looking into one of the rooms. "This was the music room," said Debbie. I peered in. It was deserted, large, but nothing to distinguish it from all the rest.

103

"How did you know this was the music room?" I asked.

"I could see the instruments--there was a harp."

I turned to a stunned Mrs. N_____. "She's right; that was the music room. Is she a relative of the Cass family?"

I shook my head. Debbie had never been to the house before.

She peered in again. "There is something here. He doesn't like what is happening to his house. He loved the place and now it's falling down."

I turned to address our guide, but was surprised to discover that she had vanished! I believe our talk of ghosts had frightened her off. She had disappeared as quietly as a phantom.

Our guide, perhaps believing us to be 'kooks' decided that it might be better to leave the tour as quietly and as quickly as possible. She vanished like a ghost down a narrow alley way.

We hoped that the present owners would repair the historic structure and put the Captain's worries over his home to rest.

I am convinced that there is life after death...
Death does not really exist.
                              --Dr. Elisabeth Kubler-Ross

The Ghosts of Mission San Miguel

I turned the car off Highway 101 into the small community of San Miguel, north of San Luis Obispo. The warm summer sun reflected brightly off windows in the 100 plus temperature. This Monday, psychic Debbie Christenson was with me again. She was to prove or disprove the rumors of ghosts at the Old Mission San Miguel Archangel.   The adobe complex of structures came into view as I pulled the car into the dusty parking lot before the plain white washedchurch. Because it was a Monday, only a few tourists were walking the grounds, making it an ideal time to conduct a psychic investigation. Debbie and I unpacked our notebooks and cameras for our investigation. She had little or no knowledge of the unique history of this Spanish mission which made her ideal to investigate the site.

We entered the gift shop and began our tour of the thick walled adobe buildings. Debbie moved slowly through the restored rooms that make up the museum section of the Mission. She was silent as we wandered the cool, dim rooms. Founded in 1791 by Fray Lasuen, the Mission's growth was marred by fire and famine. In 1844 the Mission was illegally sold to an Englishman named John Reed by Mexican Governor, Pio Pico. Reed opened the Mission buildings as an Inn during the gold rush. The inn prospered during that period as miners visited it on their travels from Los Angeles to San Francisco.

Four years later a gang of renegade English sailors chanced to stay at the Inn and heard Reed brag about his hidden gold. The tars left, ostensibly to continue their journey south, but instead they doubled back and when darkness fell, murdered Reed, his family, servants and visitors at the inn. A total of 13 were murdered that terrible night. The outlaws ransacked the premises but failed to locate Reed's hidden treasure. The sailors fled south toward Santa Barbara, but a posse, quickly formed, caught the murderers and executed them.

From that day on reports of ghosts have been told in connection with the Mission San Miguel. One specter reported time and again in the early twentieth century is that of a white dressed figure of a woman. Some believe it is the restless spirit of Mrs. Reed.

As Debbie moved out of the rooms into the courtyard she stopped and stumbled as if in pain.

"Are you all right?" I asked.

"I feel as if something just hit me in the back," she said holding her lower back. "I feel as if I had been stabbed." She leaned against a brick pillar. Debbie pulled up her shirt tail to reveal an ugly red mark or welt on her skin. "That hurts. It feels like a red hot knife," she said. She shuddered again and her eyes became wide as she looked up and down the corridor. "Blood," she said in a low voice. "Blood everywhere. On the walls, blood splattered on everything."

She held her head in pain as I led her along the archway to a bench. "Screaming. I can hear them screaming," she exclaimed. "Make them stop; it's horrible. They are killing them." She was covered with sweat. I glanced down to see Debbie's shirt stained red with blood. The wound on her back began to bleed. Debbie began to cry deeply, shaking her head as tears ran down her cheeks. "She is so lonely," Debbie said in a low voice. "She is so much in pain."

"Who?" I asked, trying to comfort her.

"She's here now." Debbie looked up at a gateway marked 'The Sheep's Gate'.

"There she is crying for her babies--they are all dead. They were murdered."

As I glanced up I noticed a misty image that filled me with dread. The image seemed to glide before the darkened gate and out into the bright sunshine of the garden. There it vanished. Was it mist I had seen or an optical illusion?

Debbie looked up and the tears had dried. "She's gone," the psychic said. "She was killed here. They were all murdered here: men, women and children. They were all buried here too in one common grave."

I checked her blouse. There was a small amount of blood, but the wound had stopped bleeding.

"There is something wrong here," she said. "They should put up a marker or a monument to the dead. They will never rest until they receive a proper burial."

Debbie, drained and exhausted, left the Mission. She had sensed the murders and physically communicated with the phantom.

Records indicate that the victims were buried in a mass grave the day after the massacre. Perhaps in the rush to bury the dead they were not given the prescribed rites.

We left the Mission convinced that the troubled spirits of San Miguel were much more than folklore. Had I seen the ghostly lady, or had my eyes deceived me? The wound on Debbie's back?

Could she have backed into a nail or suffered an insect bite? Or was she in such harmony with the ghostly lady that she suffered the same wound?

> Six weeks after his death my father appeared
> to me in a dream. It was an unforgettable
> experience and forced me--for the first time--
> to think about life and death.
>
> --Dr. Carl Jung

The Ghostly Lady of Adelaida

Ohe will be here," he assured me for the tenth time in the preceding half-hour. Many think of ghost hunting as an exciting lark; a scary walk through an old musty mansion at midnight. But in reality ghost hunting is often like a police "stakeout." It involves long hours of inactivity and boredom with only the slightest chance of encountering a fleeting apparition.

Mr. Donald K_____ of Isla Vista had encountered a ghostly lady in the cemetery at Adelaida late at night. He said that the white lady appeared on Friday night between 10:00 p.m. and midnight. It was now a crisp 11:30 and only a squirrel and several birds had been observed.

"I have seen the woman, she is always here," said Donald. "She will be here."

Donald was a college student and had a keen interest in the paranormal. He had conducted several amateur investigations before contacting me. His story of a phantom figure in the graveyard of a ghost town was all I needed to pack my bags for a nocturnal ghost watch. After meeting the lanky student at the UCSB campus we started north on Highway 101 for the ghost town located in northern San Luis Obispo County. Donald related several of his adventures as a ghost hunter.

He produced from his brief case several polaroid photos of 'ghosts' he had taken at a house in Santa Barbara. The pictures were fuzzy as if he had moved the camera. Orange spots appeared on the pictures of a house. Donald called the spots "floating orbs of energy."   "They look like reflections to me," I said. "Notice how the setting sun is reflecting in the windows." He seemed crestfallen that his ghost pictures did not impress me. I have seen hundreds like them; reflections, light leaks, scratches on the negatives and improper developing. Very few spirit photographs appear to be genuine.

I asked how he had heard of the Adelaida haunting and what he knew of the ghost town. He produced a thick pad of notes from his bag and explained that his ex-girl friend had lived in the area and had taken him to the site. He had been to the cemetery several times and after encountering the phantom had spent hours of research on the town in the historical museum in San Luis Obispo and at the local library. Consulting his numerous notes he told of the history of the old Mennonite settlement.

"The ghost is believed to be the wife of one of the local

residents of the town who lost her children to diphtheria. In her grief she would go to the cemetery every Friday to place flowers at the graves. But as she grew older she became more and more depressed until she took her own life." He turned the page and continued, "Some say she hanged herself in the old school house. Others say it was poison. Another woman who lives nearby believes that she pined away and died of self-starvation. I have one account that she and her husband moved on and that the suicide is just a story."

"What do you believe?" I asked.

"She's there all right, I've seen her," he replied. "I am sure she killed herself but I bet the family hushed it up--I mean the suicide part--back then suicide was a social no-no. It was a sin that could prevent a person from getting a proper burial. I bet they called it something else so she could receive a Christian service and burial near her children."

Hours passed as we followed Highway 101 north past San Luis Obispo and Atascadero until we reached Paso Robles. We turned west on Adelaida Road going towards Cambria.

The roadway twisted and turned into the primeval splendor of the Santa Lucia Mountains. The road was narrow with oak trees looming on one side. In places small farms could be seen, some clean and prosperous, others weatherbeaten and abandoned. The roadway followed a small creek. Here and there the oaks seemed to be hung with Spanish moss. Our journey had led us into a forgotten corner of San Luis Obispo County where a chance encounter with a horse-drawn carriage would not seem out of place.

At last we reached the weed infested graveyard and stopped the car. Dusk was settling over the quiet area and a pall of purple light seemed to give the humble cemetery a certain majesty. We unpacked our gear and opened a picnic basket I had prepared.

We discussed theories as we finished our cold dinner and planned our ghostly stakeout. I had two cameras with me as well as a powerful flashlight. Knowing I would be out late, I was dressed warmly.

Donald pointed out where he had seen the misty image which seemed to have been wearing an old-fashioned nightgown. I set up the tripod for a picture and checked the batteries of the flash unit. I spread a blanket and we sat down for an expected fruitful night. The stars slowly materialized as night slowly descended.

It was with rising interest that we watched and waited. We spoke in low whispers with long intervals of silence. But as the hours passed, nothing occurred. Donald began to describe what he had seen and assure me that the ghost would come. Our pulses raced at one point when a movement startled us: it proved to be only a bird. Hours passed, one after the other, and by 1:00 a.m. I felt rather foolish and could only laugh.

"Maybe she had a hot date tonight." suggested Donald. We took turns watching, but as I began to believe I would never be warm again, the misty wisps of dawn became visible in the east. We took a few pictures and began to pack our equipment.

"There," he screamed. I dropped my bag and saw in the graveyard near one of the ornate tombstones something that seemed to shimmer; a light or reflection. It was not shaped like a woman. It was maybe three feet tall, and had the shape of a peanut. It moved off quickly and vanished! I had seen it for about two or three seconds. Was it a reflection from one of our camera lens, a car mirror, or was it the phantom lady?

After making a check of the cemetery, we drove off for Paso Robles and a good hot breakfast. "She was there," Donald said. "You saw her--didn't she look sad?" I could only smile. It did indeed look like a sorry ghost if ghost it was.

Ghosts
of
The Channel Islands

It is wonderful that six thousand years have now elapsed since the creation of the world, and still it is undecided whether or not there has ever been an instance of the spirit of any person appearing after death. All argument is against it, but all belief is for it.

--Dr. Samuel Johnson (1709-84)

Santa Cruz

San Miguel

Anacapa

Santa Rosa

San Nicolas

N

Ghosts of The Channel Islands

1. Cabrillo's Grave
2. Ghost Lady
3. Ghost Lady
4. Indian Massacre
5. Chinese Ghost
6. Ghostly Footprints

P.P.'86

Cabrillo's Ghost

San Miguel Island, off the coast of Santa Barbara County, is a brooding windswept place. It is haunted by violent memories, tales of a wandering ghost, and a terrible curse. The island was the site of a tragedy that happened to the leader of the first European explorers in California. It was on San Miguel Island that explorer Juan Rodriguez Cabrillo died in the winter of 1543.

After the conquest of the Aztecs in Mexico the Spanish conquistadors sought new civilizations to plunder. In this spirit, two hastily constructed ships were launched on the west coast of Mexico and sent north seeking the mythical seven golden cities of Cibola. The ships were manned by a crew conscripted from the local Mexican prisons and taverns.

The small vessels were slim-hulled caravels, perhaps sixty feet long, under the command of Portugese captain and navigator, Juan Rodriguez Cabrillo.

Working their way north, against the winds, they beat their way up the coast of Baja, California making port in San Diego Bay. They found no golden cities to conquer, but discovered the Channel Islands and the coast of the Santa Barbara Channel. These Indians, called the "Chumash", inhabited all of the islands of the Santa Barbara Channel with the exception of Anacapa.

Charting the coast, Cabrillo decided to winter on San Miguel Island. It was at Cuyler Harbor, according to speculation, that the explorer fell, fracturing his upper arm. The bone ripped through the skin. The wound became gangrenous. After weeks of pain Cabrillo lapsed into a coma and died. The crew was deeply saddened by the loss of their leader. Some accounts say that they buried him in a lead casket, wearing his armor, his jewel encrusted sword at his side. He was buried in an unmarked grave out of fear his body would be disturbed by the curious natives. To this date the exact location of Cabrillo's grave is shrouded in controversial speculation. Some believe he may have been buried at Prisoner's Harbor on Santa Cruz; others suggest one of the swampy islands of the Goleta Slough as his final resting place, referring Chumash myths of an armored man.

Cabrillo's Ghost

The location of a small monument erected at Dead Man's Point on San Miguel Island is perhaps the best guess as to the burial chamber of Cabrillo. From the time of Cabrillo's burial, stories are told on windswept nights that a mournful figure wanders on the moonlit rocks. A figure glimmering with armor, a form that searches the horizon for the ships that left him so far from his native land. According to some tales he walks guarding a treasure buried with his casket. Some believe that Cabrillo cursed the Island before his fevered death. The curse vows a violent death to any who makes his permanent home on this island.

In the late 1920s a man defied the curse and operated a ranch on San Miguel. Herbert Lester took upon himself the lofty title of "King of San Miguel" and prospered for years until he was forced by the U.S. Government to leave in 1941. He shot himself rather than leave his Island home--perhaps a victim of the terrible curse of Juan Cabrillo.

Does Cabrillo's ghost wander among San Miguel's dunes and rocks? Before you scoff, spend a lonely night camped on that windy isle and listen to the howling breeze and pounding surf. Then the stories of the ghost may become more credible.

The Haunted Islands

The Channel Islands seem lonely and forlorn. They appear to be forgotten by time, truly isolated from the bustle of contemporary society. Perhaps it is this quiet that lends these islands an air of haunting mystery. The Indians who once made them their home are extinct. Disease and mass slaughter took their deadly toll. The Spanish brought dreaded European diseases along with their missions. The natives had no immunity against these new sicknesses and perished in great numbers.

The Indians who survived the onslaught of diseases were attacked by Russian fur traders with their Aleut Indian allies. The Russians came south from Alaska and Fort Ross to hunt sea otters. The fur of the otter was prized as a trade item. The Russians landed on the islands, raping women and killing natives in terrifying slaughters when conflicts occurred. For many years mounds of bones could be seen on some of the islands, mute testimony to acts of barbarism. The Spanish at the mainland missions were powerless to defend the islands from these attacks and could offer protection only to those who abandoned the islands and moved behind the walls of the missions. Many chose to remain on the islands facing possible violent death by the fur traders. Many have reported seeing ghostly figures on the islands, especially on the high places where the natives once held religious services. Strange wailings and haunting notes of a wistful flute have been heard. At dawn spectral Indians have been seen on several of the Islands on high windswept peaks, crying out to their ancient gods.

> The ghost in man and the ghost that once was man
> Are calling to each other in a dawn
> stranger than earth has ever seen.
>   --Alfred Lord Tennyson

The Chinese Ghost of Santa Cruz Island

The figure moves slowly along the rocks, his distinctive Chinese straw hat bobbing in the twilight. The phantom Chinese searches the rocks, searching perhaps until the end of time. His story is one of tragedy.

In the late nineteenth century a prosperous colony of Chinese was established on Santa Cruz Island. Their chief source of income was abalones. These mollusks were believed by the Chinese to hold the secret of longevity and the fried meat of the abalone was in great demand in the Orient. The colorful shells of the abalone were also marketable for making buttons and jewelry.

One of the Chinese abone gatherers working along the rocks of Santa Cruz caught his hand between a rock and a stubborn abalone. The pry bar he used to dislodge the mollusks fell from his hand leaving him trapped, as the tide slowly flowed in to shore. He screamed for help but his co-workers had moved on and his cries were drowned out by the roar of the pounding surf. Slowly the man realized he was faced with a horrifying choice: he could drown or amputate his own hand. He kept screaming out for help as the ocean crept higher and higher around him. Finally, he could delay no longer and taking his rusting knife he began his crude surgery.

Weakened by the terrible pain and the loss of blood he could not climb free of the rocks and the numbing sea. He lost consciousness fell and was drowned in the tide. Later his body was found and returned to his village in China for burial. But the abalone hunter's severed hand was never found. His restless ghost haunts the shores of the island in search of his lost member.

Ghosts fear men much more than men fear ghosts.
--Ancient Chinese proverb

The Footprints of Prisoners Harbor

Can ghosts leave footprints?" The noise in the room almost obscured her question.

"There are some accounts of this," I answered, "but, many believe that apparitions can not affect the real world. They are much like hallucinations. Still, no one knows for sure."

The room seemed to quiet as Mrs. R_____ looked deep into my eyes with conviction. "I saw the footprints," she confided in me, "and so did my friend. They were still wet! They were the footprints of a ghost!"

Mrs. R_____, a well-dressed professional, had attended a lecture I had given on ghosts and haunted houses and sought me out to discuss her unique experience. We sat down as I opened my notebook and took down her account.

"Where did this happen?" I asked.

"It was on Santa Cruz Island. I was with a group at Prisoner's Harbor," she began. "We were sailing around the island with a tour. We had hiked that day and our guide had been telling us the history of the Island. That night, at Prisoner's Harbor, we had a campfire and our guide told us of the Haunted Oak and the Ghost Lady of Prisoner's Harbor."

I have heard many of the stories of the Channel Islands but this was a new one to me. When asked she retold the legend: "Long ago a Chumash Indian woman was captured by the Spanish and tied to a large oak tree. The Spanish padres threatened her with death by burning if she did not renounce her tribal gods and become a Christian. She refused and was burned alive at the oak tree. As the flames rose around her body she yelled out a terrible curse upon the Spanish. It is believed that her ghost haunts the area around Prisoner's Harbor."

Acts of cruelty were recorded in the early years of Spain's occupation of the new world, but I had never heard of such horrors committed in California. The Franciscan fathers were known for not enforcing conversions, knowing that such conversions were insincere. Still the history of Prisoner's Harbor is one of such violence that atrocities conceivably could have occurred.

The small harbor is named for a prison colony that was founded there in 1830. A ship load of convicts from Mexico were taken to Santa Cruz Island and abandoned with tools, seeds, and cattle in the hope that they would build a colony. Supplies quickly ran out and a fire burned their camp. In desperation, the convicts built a large raft of driftwood and set out for the mainland. Fortune favored the castaways. They made a landing near Carpinteria and reportedly were accepted by the local population. During the months that the convict colony existed, who knows what acts were committed upon the native population? Perhaps a hapless Indian woman was burned to death.

Mrs. R_____ continued her narrative. "After telling us the story of the ghost lady, our guide said that every time newcomers came to the island the lady would walk leaving watery footprints on the small pier--going out to the end of the pier and stopping. Well, that night a friend and I went walking on the beach. As we talked, we could see the pier at all times. There was no one on the pier, I can swear to that. As a joke we decided to check the wharf for the ghost foot prints. We were shocked to find damp footprints with our flashlight. The small bare footprints lead out to sea. The prints were small, too small for the men in our group--they were the prints of a woman or child. We had been watching the pier for some time and they would have had been made within moments of our search. They were the ghost's footprints--that's the only explanation that makes sense."

I was not present at the wharf that night, but her conviction convinced me that she had experienced something out of the ordinary on Santa Cruz Island. If by chance you should visit Prisoner's Harbor late at night, walk the pier--but keep alert--for you may not be walking alone.

Santa Rosa Ghost

Sometimes she is seen as a floating ball of light drifting over the valleys of Santa Rosa Island. Others report seeing a sobbing figure wearing a wispy dress. The apparition of the Ghost Lady of Santa Rosa is believed to be the troubled spirit of a wife of a herdsman on the island who decades ago hung herself out of loneliness. Her ghostly form searches the deserted valleys seeking for her long lost husband.

The descriptions of the wandering specter are very similar to reports of "La Llorona" seen throughout the Southwest. The island ghost lady is different only in the fact that she doesn't seek human companionship. She retreats when hikers or herdsmen approach. Those that have seen the apparition tell of blowing shrouds of cloth and hair as it drifts above the ground. The fabric glides even on windless nights as if the phantom was forever trapped in a psychic whirlwind. If by chance you hike the lonely valleys of Santa Rosa Island and you see a glowing bit of light far away on the crest of a hill, you may have seen the apparition of the Ghost Lady.

Conclusion

This book covers only some of the ghosts that people have encountered wandering along the highways and biways of the haunted Gold Coast. Once ghosts were the unique province of the storyteller and theologian. More recently, ghosts have become subject to close examination by the parapsycologist and the ghost hunter.

It appears that where ever men battle for wealth and power and spill each other's blood in violence, there will be ghosts. The march of history has left a host of phantoms in its wake along the Gold Coast. Perhaps the sweep of history has left a deep scar in your neighborhood. Perhaps when the wind is crisp and the moon is full you will encounter a restless specter and you too will believe.

GLOSSARY

Apparition: A term used by psychic researchers to describe all types of visual, non-physical images.

Dematerialize: To vanish leaving no trace.   This can be sudden or accomplished as a slow vaporizing of an apparition.

ESP: The initials stand for Extra Sensory Perception.   Sight, **taste**, sound, smell, touch are the five known human senses.   Other possible senses are telepathy, psychokinesis and psychometry are classed as ESP.

Exorcism: A ritual performed to drive out a spirit from the place it is haunting.

Ghost: An apparition or manifestation encountered repeatedly at one site.

Hallucination: An image which seems real, even though it does not physically exist.

Haunted House: A house where ghosts or other psychic phenomena occur.

Haunting: A situation in which a particular place is visited over and over again by the same ghost, a kind of visual memory of an event.

Materialization: The sudden appearance of an object or image.

Medium: A person who is believed to have the ability to communicate with the spirits of the deceased.

Ouija Board: A board game believed to communicate with the dead. Name is French and German for "yes".

Parapsychology: A scientific study of psychic phenomena.

Phantom: Another term for ghost.

Planchet: Pointing device used on Ouija Board and used for automatic writing.

Psychic: A general term used to describe forces which have no physical explanation or a person who has ESP ability.

Psychic Phenomena: A term used for all psychic occurrences.

Seance: A seated group, lead by a medium that tries to communicate with the dead. Sittings of 13, that is six couples and a medium are common.

Spirit: A discarnate entity believed to be the soul of a once living person.